## What Russ Whitney's Students Say About His Training

"Our positive cash flow from our first deal [rental property] is $1,200 a month. Not to mention we walked out of closing with a check."

—Michael & Rosanna R., New York

"Wow! This is a dream come true for me. I have had an interest in real estate for over fifteen years and I even purchased other real estate programs, but I have never done anything with it until now. I'm on my way to becoming a millionaire thanks to your course."

—Dwayne O., Virginia

"I still can't believe that today I own $1.4 million in real estate and it only took fifteen months. This is forty-eight units and my cash flow is $4,500 per month."

—Karen H., Florida

"I bought a four-unit property with three finished units from an estate at $50,000 below current market price. Immediate equity! It has a cash flow of $1,700 per month."

—Hollis K., Louisiana

"Next week I will close on a thirty-two-unit apartment (should be no money down) and it generates $45K positive cash flow. I am extremely pleased with the support that I get."

—Geoffrey N., Missouri

"This past year, we have sold eight houses. The highest profit was $44,000. Once I sold in New York, sight unseen, for $36,000 profit. The education you guys gave us has been more than life changing."

—Anthony & Joan P., Florida

"Our profit at closing was $78,821! This transaction was completed within thirty-five days. We thank Russ Whitney and his power team for that. We are truly grateful."

—Ruben & Anita R., California

## What Wealth-Building Experts Say About
## *The Millionaire Real Estate Mindset*

"Russ Whitney's *The Millionaire Real Estate Mindset* contains an incredible wealth of real-world insights and powerful action steps that will change your life. Read this book, follow his advice, and watch supercharged results immediately follow."

—Mike Litman, #1 best-selling author of *Conversations with Millionaires*

"Finally! It took a straight shooter like Russ to show that real estate is not a get-rich-quick type of business. If that is what you are looking for, then put this book down. If you want to change your approach to life and real estate, then a millionaire mindset is the only means to building and maintaining a significant net worth through real estate. Russ has the credentials and integrity to change your mindset, so throw away all those other books and focus your desired change on this one."

—Frank McKinney, creator of the first nine-figure spec home and best-selling author of *Make it BIG!* and *Frank McKinney's Maverick Approach to Real Estate Success: How You Can Go from a $50,000 Fixer-Upper to a $100 Million Mansion*

"In *The Millionaire Real Estate Mindset*, Russ takes us on a journey to where all *real* wealth exists, in our mind. He shows us how to unlock the vault to our inner wealth. But he doesn't stop there—he gives the surest road map to your own MBA in (Massive Bank Account) Real Estate. This is an exciting guide to wealth."

—G. William Barnett II, best-selling author of *Are You DUMB Enough To Be RICH? The Amazingly Simple Way To Make Millions In Real Estate!*

"There are very few people who have achieved massive wealth, and of those, there are only a handful who will take the time and energy to teach you. Russ Whitney is one of those rare individuals. Read and grow rich."

—T. Harv Eker, author of the #1 *New York Times* best-selling book *Secrets of the Millionaire Mind*

"Getting rich in America today just got a whole lot easier! Russ Whitney's new book, *The Millionaire Real Estate Mindset*, is a treasure chest loaded with investment strategies that can make your dreams come true. When it comes to financial success in life, Russ Whitney is an absolute genius. This book is phenomenal!"

—Albert Lowry, Ph.D., *New York Times* best-selling author of *How You Can Become Financially Independent by Investing in Real Estate*

"One of the best books ever on real estate. It will get you to think right and do it right the first time. *The Millionaire Real Estate Mindset* is a must-read for any investor, beginner, or pro. Every page is full of great information."

—Robert Shemin, full-time real estate investor and best-selling author of *Secrets of a Millionaire Real Estate Investor*

# The Millionaire Real Estate Mindset

▼

MASTERING THE MENTAL SKILLS

TO BUILD YOUR FORTUNE

IN REAL ESTATE

## Russ Whitney

CURRENCY

DOUBLEDAY

*New York   London   Toronto   Sydney   Auckland*

A CURRENCY BOOK
PUBLISHED BY DOUBLEDAY
a division of Random House, Inc.

CURRENCY is a trademark of Random House, Inc., and
DOUBLEDAY is a registered trademark of Random House, Inc.

Cataloging-in-Publication Data is on file with the Library of Congress.

ISBN 0-385-51482-4

*Book design by Chris Welch*

First Edition: January 2006
All trademarks are the property of their respective companies.

SPECIAL SALES
Currency Books are available at special discounts for bulk purchases for sales promotions or premiums. Special editions, including personalized covers, excerpts of existing books, and corporate imprints, can be created in large quantities for special needs. For more information, write to Special Markets, Currency Books, specialmarkets@randomhouse.com.

1 3 5 7 9 10 8 6 4 2

*Dedicating a book is a very meaningful gesture for authors. Rather than giving this page a quick pass or some overused phrases, I ask myself: What is really important to me today? What is important in life? How did I come to write a book that may change the lives of tens of thousands, perhaps even hundreds of thousands of people, in a very positive way?*

*As quickly as I have the thought, the answer comes. And I know how this book should be dedicated.*

*First, to God and Jesus Christ, my personal Lord and Savior. The instant Jesus came into my heart, my life was forever changed.*

*Next, to Ingrid, my wife of twenty-nine years, who was there through all the good times and, more important, supported me through the tough times, as well.*

*To Thea, my daughter, who has grown up to make her dad and mom very proud.*

*To Russell, my son, who is now achieving his own life's dreams, as his dad and mom always knew he would.*

*And to Michael, a special, special son whom we love dearly and we know is destined for great things.*

*I love you all and thank you for all you have given me.*

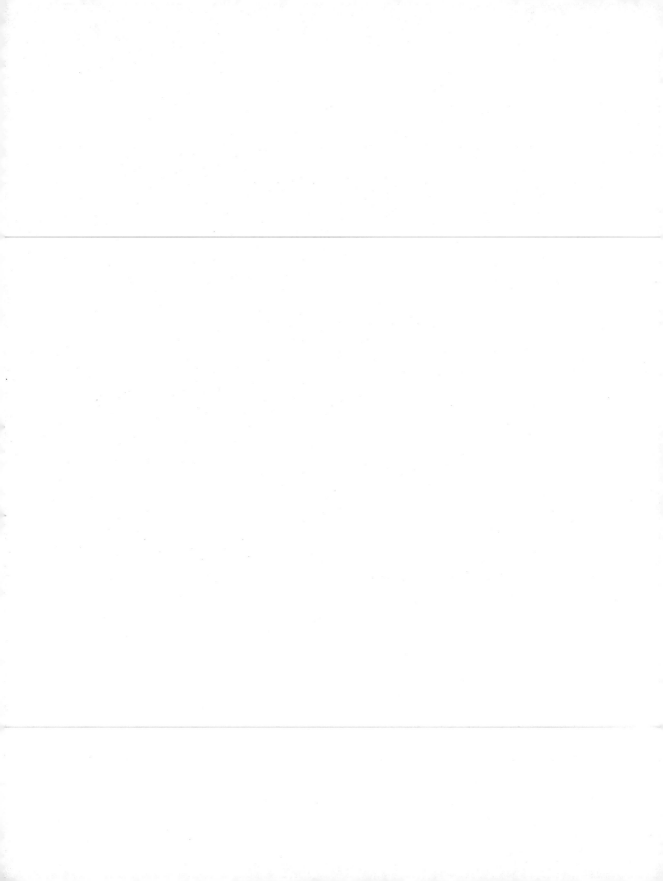

# Contents

# Acknowledgments

I've come to realize that writing the acknowledgments for a book is very similar to making an Academy Awards acceptance speech. Say too little, and the people you failed to mention might be offended. Say too much, and the audience will get bored and stop listening. It's hard to get it "just right." Even so, I want to thank the people who played a role in the creation of this book.

I begin with gratitude and praise to God and Jesus Christ, my Lord and Savior. Next, I thank my students. They have given my work a special purpose, and their success is not only my daily reward but a mission bestowed upon me by a power higher than we will ever be able to understand in this life.

Through their contribution to the company, every member of the Whitney Education Group team has also contributed to this project. Some deserve special recognition; they are: Susan Carrillo, the world's best executive assistant, whose skill at keeping me on track is phenomenal; Ron Simon; John Kane; Rick Bowers; Nick

Maturo; Tom McElroy; Marie Code; Kent Densley; Raquel Torres; Anil Singh; Marian VanDyke; and the rest of our management team.

Thanks go to my agent, Michael Baybak, for finding a great publisher for this book, and to Roger Scholl, my editor, for his guidance as we turned this vision into a manuscript.

Special appreciation goes to Jacquelyn Lynn, who assisted me in writing this book. Jackie, you are a great friend, a superb writer, and have the patience of a saint. Your never-ending patience and persistence have helped to make this a great book. Thanks. I hope we work together for many years to come.

# Preface

At any given time, there are literally hundreds of books in print and available to purchase on how to invest in real estate. Probably thousands of books have been written over the years on this topic, and they've sold millions of copies.

So why aren't more people wealthy as a result of their real estate investments?

It's not because the information isn't out there. It's not because the investment opportunities aren't out there. And it's not because it necessarily takes a lot of cash to start investing.

The reason more people haven't built their own personal fortunes with real estate—or even their own business—is simply this: They don't have the millionaire mindset.

Certainly, they'd like to be rich. They fantasize about the big house, luxury car, designer clothes, and expensive jewelry. But without the millionaire mindset, those dreams will never be anything more than elusive fantasies.

In my last book, *Millionaire Real Estate Mentor,* I explained a wide range of specific investing techniques. My goal was to give my readers enough options so that they could achieve their financial goals doing something in the real estate field that they enjoyed.

The book accomplished that. It was, and continues to be, a best-seller. Readers and reviewers tell me it's a well-written, clear guide to successful real estate investing. But there's more to building wealth than technique and strategy.

If you are going to become wealthy, you need to know more than the mechanics of whatever wealth-building vehicle you choose. You need to know how to develop your own millionaire mindset—and that means knowing how to get off the start line and win the race. It means understanding the technical side of the deals and the psychology of the process. It means knowing your own strengths and weaknesses, likes and dislikes, and figuring out what you were meant to do. It means getting past your fears and doubts and all those negative messages that have been drilled into your brain all your life so you can move forward.

The millionaire mindset isn't about the houses, jewelry, and cars. It's about something deep inside you—a self-awareness and determination that, once tapped, will make you virtually unstoppable on your road to success and wealth.

I started to develop my own millionaire mindset when I was twenty. I had a troubled youth; my mother left when I was a toddler, my father died when I was fourteen, and I dropped out of school, got in with the wrong crowd, and got into serious trouble. It was probably the best thing that ever happened to me, because I realized that I didn't want to spend my life being a victim and complaining about how unfair life is. I was able to turn my life around, and before I turned twenty-one, I knew I was going to be a millionaire many times over. I didn't completely understand it then, but I had already begun developing the millionaire mindset.

It wasn't just dreams—although I had plenty. It wasn't just having goals—although I had plenty of those, too. And I certainly didn't know *how* I was going to get where I wanted to be, but I knew I had to figure it out.

I wasn't stupid, but I *was* naive. And in retrospect, that was good, because I didn't realize that I "couldn't do" what I wanted to do. I started responding to all those "get rich" ads—the ones that promised "mail-order millions" and "build wealth while you sleep" and "make a fortune without doing a bit of work."

But I wasn't looking for a way to get rich without any effort. I knew that anything worth having was worth working for, and I didn't mind working. I just needed to find the right vehicle, and I was looking everywhere for it. Then I came across an ad for a book on how to invest in real estate. It was $10—twice my hourly wage at the slaughterhouse where I worked as a laborer. I ordered the book, and when it came, I stayed up all night reading it.

I knew instinctively that I had found what I was looking for. This was something that made sense. It didn't matter that I had been in trouble or dropped out of high school or had a wife and a baby on the way—I could do what this book taught.

And I did.

And in three weeks, I'd made $11,000 on a real estate deal—the same amount I had to work a year at the slaughterhouse to earn. I didn't spend that money on clothes, jewelry, or cars—I invested it in more real estate. That's the kind of financial-management approach that goes with the millionaire mindset.

Today, I have enough money and enough passive investments that I could stop working and never work again. My financial future is secure—and in fact, it has been for many years. But I will continue to actively invest in real estate, to work in my companies, and to manage my assets for two very important reasons: First, because that's what someone with the millionaire mindset does. Second, because in the course of my work, I get to teach people how to change their lives for the better, and I can't walk away from that.

It's that second reason that drove me to write this book. There are plenty of ways for you to learn proven wealth-building techniques, but they probably aren't going to work for you until you develop the millionaire mindset. So let me show you how to do that.

# PART 1

# The Millionaire
# Mindset

# CHAPTER 1

# Why Isn't
# Everyone Rich?

It's a question that makes perfect sense: With so many books out there on how to become wealthy, why isn't everyone rich? Why are so many bright, intelligent people struggling to get by, working jobs they hate, hoping to win the lottery? Why have so many others achieved a degree of success but can't figure out how to get where they really want to be?

Now let's take this question to a more personal level. Why aren't *you* rich? No matter how much you might have, if you don't have all the financial assets and material things you want, why not?

This book is going to help you answer that question. Even more important, it's going to help you change your situation so that you can achieve the success—financial, personal, or otherwise—that you want.

Whether you are starting with nothing, have a good-paying job and a comfortable nest egg, are a professional with a six-figure-plus income, or have a substantial investment portfolio already, I'm going to show you how to maximize what you have and get more. It doesn't matter why you want more, and I'm not passing judgment on your reasons. Some of us want the material rewards of wealth solely for the pleasure of having luxuries. Others want to make a lot of money so they can help those less fortunate. I personally have found a comfortable balance; my lifestyle is definitely comfortable, but I am also very generous with my support of worthwhile charities and other philanthropic efforts—and even friends and family members who need help. That's my choice; you'll make your own about what to do with your wealth. My goal is to help you get it.

There is absolutely no question that real estate is one of the best wealth-building vehicles available. Successful real estate investors have been sharing their techniques in books and other training materials for decades. In fact, it was a $10 book on real estate investing that taught me the techniques I used to make my first few investments.

Over the years, the real estate investment advice books became increasingly abundant. Many so-called experts—or gurus—began developing specialties. Instead of general real estate investment books, they wrote very specifically about subjects such as wholesale investing, foreclosures, mobile homes, and others.

I haven't read all of the books on real estate investing, but I've read enough of them to know that most are reasonably good and some are excellent when it comes to the specific techniques they explain. Even so, too many of the people who buy and read those books are at worst failing and at best not succeeding very well in their investments.

Most of the real estate gurus writing books these days have a fairly good grasp of the technical aspects of their subjects. But success in real estate goes much deeper than simply knowing how to find foreclosures or buy property below market value or do a profitable rehab. And these gurus aren't addressing these deeper issues that require more than technical knowledge.

So what are those books missing?

They're missing the underlying essential of building wealth, the necessary ingredient that is the millionaire mindset.

The actual process of building wealth through real estate is fairly simple. Developing the mindset of a real estate millionaire is a little more complex—but still very doable, if you know how. And knowing how will give you the power and clout to actually achieve your dreams and goals.

## Is This For You?

I love business and the business of real estate investing. I love discovering the properties, figuring out how to increase their value, negotiating the deals, working out the financing, and doing all the other things that come with this business. And that's a very important part of why I'm so successful at it. It's like playing golf, riding my motorcycle, or taking my yacht out for a day of fishing in the Gulf of Mexico—it's something I enjoy doing and have a great interest in, so quite naturally I want to do it well and always be getting better.

The way I invest in real estate has evolved significantly over the years. In the beginning, I found every property I bought myself. Today, though occasionally I do spot a property I end up buying, most of the time other people are scouting for deals and bringing them to me. I have people on my Power Team (a concept I'll explain in Chapter 8) and on my staff who handle a lot of the routine work and research necessary to put together a profitable deal. But the real point I want to make is that I enjoy every aspect of real estate investing— even the challenge of a deal that isn't working out as expected.

*To be successful at real estate investing, you need to enjoy doing it.*

If you're going to be successful at real estate investing—or at any other business, for that matter—you need to enjoy doing it. If you don't, you might be able to make a little money, but it will be very difficult for you to build real wealth.

What makes real estate such a tremendous opportunity, though, is that it really is a something-for-everyone business. There are so many different aspects to real estate investing that it's a rare person who can't find something in real estate that he enjoys, is good at, and can make money doing.

Think about what you like to do, then pick an aspect of real estate that fits your skills and personality. We'll talk more about exactly how to do that in the next chapter.

Why use real estate as a wealth-building tool? Because it works. And with real estate, while you're building your own fortune, you are providing safe, affordable housing for people, you are creating jobs, you are increasing the tax base in your community, and you might even be helping other people build their wealth by partnering with them on investments or creating real estate syndications.

Throughout history, landowners have enjoyed certain rights, privileges, and status that nonlandowners did not. Today in the United States and other developed countries, all citizens—landowners and otherwise—have the same rights, but the reality is that property owners have a degree of respect that "renters" do not. The reason for this is the inherent value attached to land. It's solid, it's lasting, and it is the foundation of wealth and power.

## Don't Count on Luck

Investing in real estate takes effort. If you're looking to get rich quick and easy, then buy lottery tickets and hope you win. But if you're counting on luck, think about this: You're working against very long odds. Remember that "lucky" rabbit's foot you're carrying didn't work too well for the rabbit.

There's a story about a fellow who desperately wanted to be rich, and he prayed every day to win the lottery. He lived in South Miami Beach and walked the beach every morning. When he would get to a particular palm tree, he would stop and talk to God. "God, how come you never let me win the lottery?" he would ask. "I want to win. I need to be more comfortable. Why won't you make my life better?"

*Millionaires don't depend on luck or hopes or wishes.*

Sometimes he would bargain with God. "God, if you'll just let me win the lottery, I'll do so much good with it. I'll give to charity. I'll help people," he would promise.

Finally, one day as he stood by the tree and begged God to let him win the lottery, God spoke. "I've heard your prayers," God said. "Help me out here. Buy a ticket."

If you want to win the lottery, you've got to buy a ticket. If you want to be successful, you've got to do the work. The late comedian Flip Wilson put it this way: "You can't expect to hit the jackpot if you don't put a few nickels in the machine."

Let me be very clear here: I'm not suggesting that anyone depend on the lottery or any other type of gambling to secure their financial future. But even lottery winners had to buy a ticket— they had to get in the game.

Trust me, millionaires don't depend on luck or hopes or wishes. If you're willing to learn what you need to do, and then do what's necessary, you can build substantial wealth and do it fairly quickly—and your chances of success taking that route are probably a million times greater than buying lottery tickets.

## What's Your Passion?

Passion and the millionaire mindset go hand in hand. Whatever you decide to do to build wealth, you must *want* to do it. You need to be passionate about it. You should enjoy doing it so much that you would do it even if you weren't making money.

This is not to say that you'll never have to do anything that you find unpleasant or uninteresting. But your passion will get you through those tasks that you would rather not have to do.

## Make Your Hour Worth More

As an investor or business owner, your time can be worth far more than any wage you might earn as an employee. It's the same hour; it has sixty minutes like every other hour. But as an employee, you're limited to earning whatever wage you've negotiated. As an investor or business owner, there is absolutely no limit to what you can earn per hour.

The reality is: No matter how much passion you have, if you work in a convenience store for $6 an hour, and that's all you do, you'll never get rich. If you are passionate about working in a convenience store, don't just get a job in one—buy one and reap the full profits.

If your passion is criminal justice, you can go to law school and get a job in the public defender's office for $50,000 a year. Or you can go to law school and do criminal defense work along the lines of high-profile attorneys such as F. Lee Bailey, Robert Shapiro, or the late Johnnie Cochran and make millions of dollars a year. It's just a matter of making your time more valuable.

*Look for ways to make the same amount of money—or more—in less time.*

When it comes to real estate investing, choose the aspect of real estate that fits your passion, learn it thoroughly, then increase the profitability of your deals to increase your earnings. For example, you might start out investing in low-income, single-family housing and be passionate about the process of finding good deals on distressed property, supervising the fix-ups, and then selling the houses. As a beginning investor, you might spend 80 to 120 hours on an average deal and clear $5,000 to $10,000. That's good, but it's not great—and it's not real wealth.

Once you master the basic investing techniques, look for ways to make the same amount of money—or more—in less time. Or figure out how to make more money in the same amount of time. That's the millionaire mindset: Take your passion and make your hour worth more money.

## The Law of Cause and Result

Understanding the law of cause and result is critical to successful wealth-building. The concept is simple: Money is a result, not a cause, of what you do. A lot of people get into a certain type of business for the money. They don't take the time to think about whether they are actually going to like doing the business, whether they have the skills and background required, or if they're going to be willing to put in the effort to educate themselves about the business. They see those dollar signs, and they leap in.

Those who have gotten involved with a network (or multilevel) marketing company understand this. When I ask my students if they've ever signed up to be a distributor for an MLM company, most of the hands in the room go up. When I ask who is getting residuals a year later, virtually all of the hands go down.

The reason these—and others—failed at network marketing doesn't have to do with the product. In fact, it's quite common for products sold through MLM to be of higher-than-average quality. And MLM companies are just like all other companies—some are well-funded, well-organized, and strong; others do not have the infrastructure needed to support the organization.

The primary reason so many people fail at network marketing businesses is the law of cause and result. They don't want to have to do what it takes to succeed in a network marketing company. It's not because they're lazy or unmotivated or not smart enough; it's because they don't want to have to pitch the product and the opportunity to everybody they meet, and they don't know what to do after they run out of friends and relatives to sell to and still have a garage full of lotions or vitamins or whatever. They get into the business dazzled by how much money they can make, not because they genuinely want to sell whatever the product is.

When your cause is making money, the result of your efforts rarely will be profits. If your cause is doing a worthwhile business very well, money becomes the natural result.

This applies to more than just network marketing businesses. How many times have you read an article on "today's hottest, most profitable businesses" and thought that you should give one of them a try because they're all so lucrative? And if you actually did try them, how long did it take you to find out that it's very, very hard to make money when you're doing something you don't want to do?

When you do something because you love it and have a passion for it—when you are willing to learn how to do it in the best possible way—the money is a natural result. The evidence is clear when you look at lists of wealthy people: Bill Gates loves working with technology and actively participates in a team of software developers. The late Sam Walton loved retailing. Oprah Winfrey loves entertaining and informing people. Thanks to the Harry Potter series, author J. K. Rowling is a billionaire; she keeps writing because she loves it. Sure, these people are making millions of dollars, but they're not working for the money. They're doing what they do because they love it, because they're passionate about it.

Another element of the law of cause and result is time. There is no such thing as an overnight success. Tiger Woods is a celebrity worth millions today, but he started playing golf when he was two years old. Arnold Schwarzenegger started working out with weights when he was a teenager. If you love what you do, you have to be willing to invest the time to learn how to do it well, then keep on doing it so you can get better at it. When you do so, the rewards will come.

## Get the Education You Need

I have been teaching people how to invest in real estate for more than twenty-five years. With both investing and teaching, I do it a lot better now than I did when I first started. And the most important thing I've learned over the years is how critical the right education is for successful real estate investing.

Many of the so-called gurus or self-proclaimed experts out there would like you to believe that all you have to do is buy their book or listen to their tapes or attend one weekend seminar, and you'll know all you need to know to make millions investing in real estate.

Let's examine the truth behind that line of thinking. Let's say you were shopping in a retail store and one of the display fixtures fell on you. The store is balking at paying your medical bills. You decide to hire an attorney to represent you, and perhaps file suit against the store if you can't negotiate a satisfactory settlement. You meet with a lawyer, who assures you that your case is strong. You like this attorney, and you ask about his credentials.

"Oh," he says cheerfully, "I went to a three-day seminar on how to be a lawyer. I'm sure I can do this."

You'd be out the door pretty fast, don't you think?

Or let's say you need heart bypass surgery. When you ask the surgeon about his education and experience, he or she says, "I bought a set of books and tapes on how to do bypasses. Let's get you into the operating room."

Do you think you'd willingly get on that operating table?

Do you know of any profession where you can earn an annual income of six figures or more that you can learn in a weekend seminar? I don't. Electricians need 7,000 to 8,000 hours of classroom and on-the-job training. Butchers need 4,000 hours. Hairdressers need 1,500 to 2,000 hours of training before they can become licensed. These are jobs that can provide a living but aren't likely to generate the serious wealth that you can amass from real estate.

*No one's education is ever complete.*

So why would anyone think they could learn everything they need to know about investing in real estate in three days? Or from one book and a set of audiotapes or CDs?

When I started investing in real estate, I had read one book. I used one technique from that book and made $11,000 in three weeks—pretty good money for a twenty-year-old who was killing hogs for $5 an hour. But I knew I didn't know it all. I figured if reading one book could get me that much money, then reading a lot of books would teach me how to make a lot more money. So I read more books, took action based on what they taught, and I made more money. Intuitively, I understood that I needed more education than just one book could provide, and at that time, there was no other place to get that kind of real estate investing education except books. I also understood that I needed to know more than just the specific techniques of how to put together a real estate deal—I needed to know how to run a business, how to sell, how to manage people, how to negotiate, and how to manage my money after I'd made it. So I read books on those subjects. My point? The millionaire mindset recognizes the power and value of education.

Let me discuss another misperception of education. Let's say you spend four or five years obtaining a college education; do you suddenly go from uneducated to educated on the day you receive your degree? Of course not. You begin learning from day one, and you build on what you've learned course after course. And you don't stop learning after you graduate. Self-made millionaire and now full-time philanthropist Sir John Templeton once said, "Wherever we are and whatever we are doing, it is possible to learn something that can enrich our lives and the lives of others. . . . No one's education is ever complete." I would amend that slightly: No one's education is ever complete *if* they are striving to grow and get better.

The same principles apply to becoming a millionaire real estate investor. You start with the fundamentals, and when you've mastered those skills, you move up to more complex techniques. You attend a class, practice what you learned, work with a mentor, attend more classes, invest in books and CDs by various authors and experts, try different techniques, study your results, and continue to refine your skills and expand your knowledge base.

## Put Your Mind on a Diet

I am a product of the self-help industry. So are many, many other millionaires and billionaires. There's more to it than just learning a few workable techniques to make money. I call it *mindfeed*: We feed our minds every day with good information. We study other wealthy people to understand how they built their fortunes, how they run their companies, how they manage their money and investments. We read books and magazines with positive, worthwhile content. Just as we take care of our bodies with good diet and exercise, we feed our minds with healthy information.

Here's what those who want to become wealthy *don't* do: We don't waste our time watching pointless dramas or reality shows on television. We don't listen to or read gossip. We reject negativity.

*Feed your mind with good information every day.*

Yes, we do take the time to enjoy good entertainment—perhaps a good film, play, novel, or sports event—and recreation, but we make sure the things we do to relax are positive and uplifting at the same time. When we read the newspaper, we skip past the stories about rapes, murders, and car crashes and focus on the business information we can use. This is a habit that all successful people—whether they are self-made millionaires or born to wealth—have learned.

Do you need to know what's going on in the world? Of course. But you need to know what's going on only to the extent it has an impact on your life, your community, and your business.

There's an old saying in newsrooms: "If it bleeds, it leads." In other words, the ugliest, most depressing, most shocking visual story is told first or on the front page, because it gets people's attention.

Watch the local six-o'clock news for a few weeks and you'll be afraid to drive your car for fear of getting in a wreck, afraid to go into a bank for fear of getting shot during a robbery, afraid you're going to catch some dreadful disease, and afraid you're going to lose your money and live the rest of your life in poverty. It's amazing that no matter how good the economic news really is, the media have a way of presenting it so that it sounds depressing. Even the so-called entertainment offered through most television networks and Hollywood movies is nothing more than mental junk food.

The truth about junk food is that it doesn't hurt you to eat fried food or candy once in a while. It's when you make that your steady diet that your body suffers. The same is true of mental junk food.

In conjunction with the process of mindfeed, I incorporate the process of *mindcleanse*. In other words, I try to clean out and get rid of all the negative concepts that have been planted in my brain over the years. When you practice positive mindfeed, mindcleanse is a natural result.

Let me compare the process again to diet. If you eat and drink high-fat, high-calorie foods that are low in nutrients, your body will reflect it. You'll gain weight, your cholesterol will skyrocket, your blood sugar will be high, and your overall health will likely be poor. But if you switch to a healthy diet of fresh foods, with plenty of fruits and vegetables and dishes that are high in important nutrients, you will cleanse your body. Your health will improve, your weight will drop, you'll lower your cholesterol and blood sugar, and you'll feel better.

The same thing will happen to your mind. As you gradually replace all the mental junk food you've been consuming over the years with positive, productive information, you will cleanse your mind. When you spend your time reading the right motivational and self-improvement books, attending classes on wealth-building, studying business and management, and doing other things that are good for your attitude and mental well-being, you'll see positive results in how you feel and how you act.

Bottom line? Find something you love to do, learn how to do it well, practice mindfeed, and you will be well on your way to developing what I call the millionaire mindset.

▼

# CHAPTER 2

# Finding Your
# Real Estate Niche

I can't say this enough: Real estate is one of the fastest, simplest, and most secure ways to build wealth. Are there other ways to make money? Of course. I've made money investing in stocks and other financial instruments. I've also started businesses of my own and invested in other companies. But the foundation of my wealth is real estate, and it always will be.

Why should you invest in real estate? Think about this: If you could pick up a newspaper from 1975 or even 1985 and look at the stock pages, many of the companies listed don't exist today. But that brick house on the corner you used to pass on your way to school is probably still there. And if it isn't, the land is. The point is: Real estate lasts. It will be here long after we're gone. It's also a finite commodity. Mark Twain once said, "Buy land. They're not making it anymore."

Another reason real estate is a good investment is leverage. Let's say you bought a four-unit apartment building for $200,000 and put

$10,000 down. If that property appreciates just 4 percent in the first year, you've made a return of 80 percent on your cash investment—and that doesn't include the rental income the property brought in.

The phrase "investing in real estate" covers a broad spectrum of strategies, techniques, and types of property. I recommend that you choose one or two types of real estate investing, learn them well, and focus your energies on them. In other words, become a specialist. Think about it: Specialists almost always make significantly more money than generalists. A neurosurgeon makes more than a family-practice doctor. Board-certified attorneys usually charge significantly more per hour than non-board-certified lawyers. When you specialize, you are able to become an expert in the one or two areas of real estate that you enjoy, and your transactions will likely be smoother and more profitable. It's unrealistic to expect that you'll be able to keep current with every aspect of every type of real estate investing—becoming a specialist is part of developing the millionaire mindset.

## Plenty of Choices

Before you can choose what type of real estate investing to do, you need to know what your options are. There are two key reasons for this: First, you want to choose something that you'll enjoy; second, you'll want to know enough about other types of investing so you can take advantage of unexpected opportunities that drop in your lap.

Think about how we educate doctors. When they're in medical school, they learn the basics of anatomy, chemistry, and all the other things every doctor needs to know. With that foundation, they go on to learn about all the various medical specialties—surgery, dermatology, oncology, obstetrics, pediatrics, and so on.

Once they have enough knowledge of each specialty to make a decision, they choose the one that is the best fit for them and direct their training accordingly. I met a pediatrician once who said he started medical school with the very focused goal of becoming a surgeon, but his pediatrics rotation changed his mind. That's why medical training is set up the way it is—so doctors can make a sound decision when they choose their specialties.

The successful real estate investors I know take the same approach. They learn the basics, then they learn a little bit about the various specialties, then they decide what they want to do and focus their education and energies in that direction.

It's possible you'll invest in learning a particular real estate investment strategy only to decide that it's not something you want to do. And that's not a bad way to invest your time and money. You can't really know whether or not you want to do something until you understand it—in some cases, you won't know until you've actually tried it. That's why traditional colleges and universities have a standard "add/drop" period at the beginning of each semester; they give students who figure out that they're in the wrong class a chance to change without penalty. And how many people do you know who changed their college major at least once and probably more than that? Or the people who have degrees but have never done any type of work in that area? Some people might say their education was wasted, but I disagree. Education is never wasted, even if all you learn is that you don't want to do something.

## Work Can—and Should—Be Fun

No matter how long you live, life is short. There is no one who has so much time that he should be willing to spend it doing something he dislikes.

This scenario is probably familiar: You go to a store, and as you're checking out, you say, "How are you?" to the clerk. And the clerk answers, "I've got another hour to work, then I'm off and I'll be great." Or you probably know people who just endure Monday through Friday to get to the weekend so they can spend their time doing something they enjoy.

*You should wake up every day excited about what you're going to do.*

Life is too short to live that way. You should wake up every day excited about what you're going to do—by every day, I mean *every* day, seven days a week, not just Saturdays and Sundays. And you shouldn't spend your working time watching the clock in anticipation of the moment when you can escape from work. An old Jewish proverb says, "Whoever enjoys his life is doing the creator's will."

I've already told you to find something you're passionate about. And you're probably thinking, *Sure, that's easy for you to say and a lot harder for everybody else to do.*

I'm not promising you that this process is effortless. In fact, it's quite the opposite. You have to work at it. But you have to work at something, so why not work at finding a way to make your living and build wealth that you genuinely enjoy doing?

I just can't imagine what the last thirty years would have been like for me if I had been working at a job I hated. But I love what I do, so I get up early—weekdays and weekends—to do it. I stay at the office late. When you do something you love, you'll do it more. When you do it more, you'll get better at it. And when you get better at it, you make more money.

## Not Just Training—the *Right* Training

I own outright or have an interest in more companies than we can list here. I start, buy, or invest in businesses because I enjoy the process *and* because I enjoy what the particular businesses do. I love driving past a neighborhood and knowing that my development company created the concept and my construction company built the houses. I love looking at a city skyline and picking out the buildings I own or have an interest in. I love creating something from virtually nothing, which is what happens when you develop raw land. And I love helping other people become wealthy.

One of my most visible operations is Whitney Education Group, a worldwide financial training company. Every month, between 40,000 and 60,000 people register for one or more of our programs—and every one of those people is a unique individual with his or her own particular goals and training requirements.

That's why the training Whitney Education Group offers is modeled after conventional postsecondary education and has been very carefully structured to maximize our students' investments of time and money while still giving them the education they need to succeed. Our real estate students (we also offer programs in stock investing, financial management, and business) start with a three-day basic course that is essentially an introduction to all types of real estate investing. From there, they go on to take additional training in the areas that appeal to them, and those courses are strategically spaced over a period of one to three years so the student is able to master each technique before going on to the next.

Students who commit to this type of education program definitely have the millionaire mindset. They understand the importance of knowledge, training, and of building on a solid foundation. They're also able to recognize their mistakes and learn from them.

Here's a scenario we've seen many times: A student goes through the initial training and gets excited about a particular strategy—let's say preforeclosures—because they can see how lucrative it is. So they take an advanced training course to learn more about how to invest in preforeclosures and foreclosures. The vast majority of students complete the training, implement the strategies, and build their portfolios. But there are always a few who say, "Whoa! This isn't what I thought it would be." Maybe they didn't realize how much research is involved in foreclosures, and they don't like doing that. Or they're not comfortable dealing with sellers who are in that situation. Foreclosure investors have to be able to deal with the emotional and financial issues the property sellers are facing and help them work through to a solution.

So some students, after learning what they need to do to invest in foreclosures, will decide they need to focus on a different strategy, such as wholesale or rehabbing. But they know how to do foreclosures, so if they happen upon an opportunity, they know what to do—just as a neurosurgeon could deliver a baby in an emergency.

In other situations, students may be interested in a particular strategy only to find out it doesn't work in their geographic location. For example, there are places where not even the most savvy real estate investor could make a living doing foreclosures—because there just aren't any. Cape Coral, the city where I live, is a classic example. We have very few foreclosures here. There are more across the river in Fort Myers, but still not a lot. By contrast, in Atlanta or Chicago, there are more foreclosures than the investors in the area can handle.

*Recognize what you don't know, then learn it.*

Part of learning about real estate investing includes learning about your market. This is not something anyone else can do for you. You have to study your own market, identify the trends in specific areas, and recognize the opportunities. When you have the millionaire mindset, you'll understand that this is not an excuse for failure, it's a way to expedite success.

There's a great Yiddish proverb that says, "The luck of an ignoramus is this: He doesn't know that he doesn't know." Don't be an ignoramus. Recognize what you don't know, then learn it.

## Know Your Business DNA

You've heard the term *DNA*. The technical name for DNA is deoxyribonucleic acid, and it carries a cell's genetic information and hereditary characteristics. Your physical DNA is a unique identifier—it can tell anyone who knows how to read it who you are.

Your business DNA is not so scientific, but it is also a unique identifier. Your business DNA is who you are and how you operate in business and investing.

When it comes to business style, there are two basic types of people: There are the very organized, detail-oriented people I call the "*i*-dotters and *t*-crossers." They want everything in its proper place. They do their research, and if they don't know all there is to know about something, they're not comfortable moving forward.

Then there are the impetuous types, those I call the "ready, fire, aim" folks. They're willing to take more chances, to kick up a little dust, to jump right in and figure things out as they go.

Both of these types can be successful investing in real estate, but they will do it differently. They have different DNA. And they need to find investment vehicles that suit their particular DNA.

Make a list of the ways you enjoy spending your time. Think about the work you've done that you liked—the work you would have done whether you got paid or not. Think about your hobbies. Why do you enjoy them and how can you find the same motivation in a for-profit activity?

Do you enjoy helping people solve their problems? Consider investing in foreclosures. Do you dislike routine and like to interact with a lot of different people? Owning and managing rental property—either residential or commercial—may suit your DNA. Do you prefer crunching numbers rather than negotiating deals? Tax lien certificates may be your match.

Take the time to figure out what aspect of real estate investing matches your particular DNA. Don't worry about the money— what's more important is that you do something you can be passionate about.

Can you make tens of thousands of dollars working just a day or two in a foreclosure deal? Sure. But if you don't enjoy the process, the money doesn't matter. You can make the same amount of money in a variety of other real estate investments. Find the one that you would do even if you weren't making any money. That's the investment that suits your business DNA.

## Real Estate Strategies That Work

Something I often hear is "I'd like to invest in real estate, but I don't want to . . ." and then whoever is speaking goes on to list all the things they don't like to do. You can use that as an excuse for not investing and not getting wealthy, or you can figure out what you like to do and find an aspect of real estate that matches. Here are some of the basic strategies to consider:

### Wholesale Buying

Buying wholesale means paying substantially below market value for properties. The conventional perception of wholesale real estate is of houses that are vacant, abandoned, and boarded up. It's true you can make substantial money dealing in those kinds of properties, but you can also buy nicer homes, multi-unit residential properties, and even commercial and industrial property at wholesale.

To buy at wholesale, you need to be able to see what others can't. For example, termite damage usually scares off buyers, but it shouldn't. It takes an infestation of ten or fifteen years before termites can do irreparable damage. Years ago, I found a house that had severe termite damage in the supporting beams in the basement. I inspected the house carefully and was sure that the termites had not done any other damage. Replacing the beams would not be particularly complicated or expensive, but apparently other potential buyers didn't see that. The property had been on the market for quite a while, so I was able to buy it at a wholesale price. I pulled money out of the property up front when I did the repairs and then made a substantial profit a few years later when I sold it.

In Chapter 11, we'll talk more about wholesaling and the specific strategies I recommend.

## Foreclosures

Investing in foreclosures includes buying property from homeowners facing foreclosure, buying the property at auction, and buying from the lender after the foreclosure. As a foreclosure investor, you can take an unfortunate situation and turn it into a win-win situation for everyone involved—and make money while you help people.

Your biggest competitor in foreclosures is not other investors, it's bankruptcy. When someone decides to file bankruptcy and walk away from their house, you can't help them. But if you can get to them before they reach that point, you may be able to stop the foreclosure, and at the same time help them salvage their credit rating and get their life back on track. Every foreclosure investor I know can talk for hours about the various people they've helped and how grateful those people are.

There are three ways to invest in foreclosures: preforeclosure (when the lender has begun the foreclosure process but you buy the property before the actual foreclosure takes place); at a foreclosure auction; or after the auction, when you can buy the property from the lender if it didn't sell, or possibly from the investor who bought it at the auction.

You can find foreclosures by reading the legal notices in your local newspaper. The foreclosure notice will tell you the address and/or legal description of the property, the owner, and when and where the property is scheduled to be auctioned. Study the foreclosure notices and get comfortable with their language and style.

When you see a foreclosure notice for a property you're interested in, make a personal visit to talk to the owner. Go to the door and ask for the owner by name. If the thought of walking up to a house and asking for a total stranger by name scares you, that's okay. It scares most people. But the fact that you're willing to do something like this will give you a serious edge over other foreclosure investors—and it's an indication that you have the millionaire mindset. Remember, successful people are willing to do what unsuccessful people won't.

At the door, *don't* say, "Hey, Mr. Jones, I saw in the paper that you're being foreclosed on. Want to sell me your house?" Be discreet. Introduce yourself and say something like, "I'm interested in buying a home in this area, and I've been told this house might be for sale." You'll get a variety of responses, from complete denial to a free admission that the house is in foreclosure. Once the owner has acknowledged his situation, tell him you think you can help him. Then sit down and go over the numbers to see if you can make a deal work.

If he doesn't want to talk, leave your card and some information behind and tell him to call you if he has any questions. Then follow up with mail or phone calls every week or two until the auction date. It's common for owners to not take action until the last minute; in fact, most preforeclosure deals take place in the last week or so before the auction date. But you should establish your relationship with the owners early so they're comfortable with you and will call you when they realize they have to sell.

If the owner doesn't sell, the property goes to auction. Attend a few auctions before you're ready to bid to see how they work and get comfortable with the process. Do as much research on the property before the auction as you can so you know what you can pay and still make a profit—and then don't bid over that amount. I also recommend bidding only on vacant properties when you're buying at auction, because it's not uncommon for the owners to trash the house during the period between receiving the order to vacate and the time they have to be out.

If the house didn't sell at auction, it reverts to the lender. Contact the lender with an offer quickly, before the property is turned over to a real estate agent. If the house sold, contact the buyer—it will usually be another investor—and make an offer.

The numbers on a foreclosure deal have to work just as they do on any other real estate deal. Figure your costs (acquisition, fix-up, etc.), your plans for the property, and what the seller wants and needs. If you can't put together a deal that's profitable for you, walk away.

## Purchase Options

Options are a smart and simple way to control property, especially high-priced real estate, with little or no cash, and often without taking ownership. The biggest challenge in using options is that most people don't understand them; you have to be able to explain them clearly so the buyers, sellers, and real estate agents you deal with will feel comfortable using the technique.

An option is essentially a one-way right to purchase property under specified terms. Only the seller is required to perform; the buyer has a choice. This strategy is so powerful that we're going to discuss it in greater detail in Chapter 12.

## Property Management

If you're going to own real estate for any length of time, you need to know how to manage it. You may want to build a substantial inventory of rental units, or you may decide that you will own only enough units to generate the positive cash flow you want.

Good landlords usually enjoy working with people. They're also organized and have strong administrative skills. There is nothing routine or boring about managing property; it's interesting, exciting, and very rewarding.

Worried that you might not be able to find tenants? Don't be. Prospective tenants are literally everywhere. To locate them, run ads, put up signs, post notices at schools and churches, contact your local housing authority, put out flyers, and offer referral fees to your existing tenants. With just a little effort, you'll have more tenants than you have properties to fill.

Screen your tenants carefully. It's much easier to decline to rent to someone who will be a bad tenant than to let him in and have to evict him later on. Ask prospective tenants to complete a rental application (see Appendix B) and tell them you're going to conduct a credit and criminal background check. In many cases, simply telling someone who has a poor history that you're going to do this will stop him from applying. You can charge an application fee—typically in the range of $25 to $40—to cover your costs. Always find out where tenants are living now and why they are moving.

Ask to see a legal photo ID and make a copy of it for your files. And check references, including at least one or two landlords other than the current one. It's not unheard of for a landlord to say good things just to get rid of a bad tenant, so go back to previous landlords to be sure you're getting an accurate reference.

When you get good tenants, work hard to keep them. Keep your properties maintained and respond to tenant requests promptly. Treat your tenants with respect; learn and use their names; remember their birthdays with a card or even a small gift; and offer referral fees if they recommend one of your properties to someone they know.

*Maintain your properties well and treat your tenants with respect.*

Most landlords charge late fees when the rent isn't paid on time. I have always found that taking a more positive approach works better. Instead of charging $700 a month in rent and a $50 fee if the rent isn't paid by the third, I set the rent at $750 and give a $50 discount if it's paid by the first.

Look for ways to make your properties as profitable as possible. Be sure your rents are in line with the market. When leases come up for renewal, evaluate the terms and raise the rent if appropriate. Give tenants written notice of a rent increase at least sixty days in advance and explain the reason for the increase (perhaps property enhancements, increased costs, or simply that the increase is in line with the market). A small percentage of tenants will move. If they do, you just replace them with a tenant paying the higher rate. Most understand price increases—and also understand that moving is probably going to be a lot more expensive than paying a modest rent increase. If you have multi-unit buildings, consider adding coin-operated washers and dryers; vending machines that dispense detergent, soft drinks, and snacks; and, if you have room, storage units that you rent to tenants for an extra fee.

Keep complete and accurate records. Set up separate files on each tenant and rental unit. The documents you should keep include leases, move-in and move-out inspections, maintenance records, copies of correspondence, and notes of any conversations. Follow basic accounting procedures in tracking income and expenses.

Once you have a system set up to manage your own property, consider offering your services as a property manager to other investors for a fee.

## Commercial Real Estate

If houses and small apartment buildings don't appeal to you, consider the more complex arena of commercial real estate. You can build wealth buying, selling, and managing office buildings, retail centers, and industrial facilities. It's helpful, but not essential, for you to have some residential experience before moving into commercial properties.

A commercial property is one that is zoned for commercial use. When you think commercial real estate, you might envision huge shopping malls, downtown office towers, or sprawling industrial parks. But a commercial property could just as easily be a small professional office building or a neighborhood retail center, and it may not cost much more than a house in a good area.

Even so, the issue of zoning creates some important differences between commercial and residential properties. The deals are generally more complex than residential transactions, with more people involved, and often higher dollar figures. There may be regulatory issues to consider, and commercial leases are far more complicated than residential rental agreements. But many of the same basic principles still apply—you need to buy at a good price, then rent for positive cash flow or sell at a profit.

The types of real estate you'll deal with in this arena are generally commercial (or retail); industrial; professional (office space); and multi-tenant or multifamily residential (large apartment buildings or complexes). Select a specialty and focus on that; don't try to work in all of these types of properties.

Start shopping for commercial real estate long before you are ready to buy. Let the sellers and brokers educate you about the investment process, the local market, and even commercial property management. Keep in mind that determining the value of a commercial property is more challenging than doing the same with residential real estate, because you aren't likely to have much, if anything, in the way of "comps" (what people have been willing to pay for comparable properties in the area recently). It's difficult to find true comps in commercial real estate because you might have several retail properties very close together but so totally different in size and amenities that there is really no comparison. The same thing could easily apply to industrial and professional space. It might be easier to find comps in multi-tenant residential, but none of these types of properties tends to turn over the same way residential real estate does. The most important factor in determining the value of a commercial property is its net income. The higher the net income, the more the property will be worth.

You should also be aware of the capitalization rate, or "cap rate," which is a ratio used to estimate the value of income-producing properties. It's essentially the rate at which you'll earn money on the property. The cap rate is expressed as a percentage and determined by dividing the net operating income (NOI) by the sales price or value. Do not include the mortgage; do this calculation as though you paid cash for the property. Commercial real estate brokers, appraisers, and lenders can tell you what the cap rate for a given area is.

Your best strategy for investing in commercial real estate is to start with residential, learn the business, develop your knowledge and skills, then venture into the commercial arena with some smaller properties before moving on to bigger deals.

## Real Estate Notes

Notes, or "paper," are the financial side of real estate transactions. These are the mortgages that are created when real estate is used as the collateral for a loan, and creating them and selling them can be extremely lucrative. Notes are a great opportunity for people who don't enjoy the process of buying, selling, and renting property but who want to invest in real estate.

A real estate or mortgage note is a promise to pay that is secured by real property. Though mortgage notes are generally created by banks or mortgage companies, plenty of them are created by individuals who are willing to act as a lender in a real estate transaction. These are known as privately held notes, and it's when that individual decides she's tired of collecting payments and wants a lump sum of cash that you come in. You can buy the note at a discount (that is, less than the balance of the loan) and collect the remaining payments yourself. Or you can broker the note to a funding source and earn a commission for your efforts.

The simplest way to find privately held notes is by searching the public records at the courthouse. When you see a property and the note holder is an individual name or even two names (e.g., Mary Jones or George and Susan Green), you have a prospect. Contact the note holder and ask if he is interested in selling the note for a lump sum of cash. If he is, get all the information about the note (property type, date of origination, original loan amount, current balance, monthly payments, interest rate, lien position, loan-to-value ratio, and other details that could affect the value of the note) and either calculate what you're willing to pay for the note or take the deal to a funding source for a quote. Present your offer to the note holder and negotiate as necessary. Just as in real estate, the note holder may be excessively demanding; if you can't make money on the deal, walk away.

If your offer is accepted, you'll go through a closing process very similar to what's required to close on a real estate deal. Your funding source will handle most of this and guide you through it.

## Mobile Homes and RV Parks

An often overlooked but proven profitable segment of the real estate market is manufactured and mobile homes. They cost less to buy but can often generate as much, or more, cash flow as a site-built home. You can buy and sell the homes, or develop and operate a manufactured/mobile home or RV park.

The terms *mobile home* and *manufactured home* are often used interchangeably, but there is a technical difference. Both are mobile housing units (although they are built with wheels and can be moved, they rarely are), but mobile homes are those built before June 15, 1976, and manufactured homes are those built after June 15, 1976. Both are different from *modular homes*, which is the term for factory-built housing designed for permanent installation.

Mobile and manufactured homes are popular as retirement homes, seasonal second homes, and even primary homes for young families and those in low- and middle-income brackets. Though these units account for approximately 10 percent of the housing stock in the United States, you won't find them in every market. You're not likely to see mobile homes in large established metropolitan areas, but they're common in younger, smaller cities, the suburbs, and rural areas. If you have a market for mobile homes in your area and the strategy interests you, start by touring parks, talking to managers, answering some "For Sale" or "For Rent" ads just for practice, and visiting dealers to see what's available in new and used homes.

Mobile homes are not real estate; they are vehicles and must be licensed, taxed, titled, and financed as such. With a little study and practice, you'll be able to evaluate a used mobile home for condition and market value. The resale book published by the National Automobile Dealers Association (NADA) will help (you can also visit www.nadaguides.com). For maximum profitability, avoid mobile homes that are in bad shape and need extensive rehab. There are plenty out there that can be purchased for a great price and need only cosmetic fix-up.

You can invest in mobile homes using the same strategy that you would for single-family site-built homes, or you can operate a mobile home park where you rent the lots to other mobile home owners. As the park owner, you may also have your own rental units available. Operating a mobile home park is in many ways similar to managing a multi-unit apartment building. You need to keep the facilities clean and well maintained, consider offering various amenities (which, depending on the size of the park, can include a clubhouse, laundry facilities, swimming pool, playgrounds, other recreation facilities, extra storage, or whatever else might appeal to the tenants in your market), and generally apply good management practices.

## Rehabbing and Renovation

If you like to work with your hands or manage construction projects, you can make money rehabbing and renovating your own properties or doing the work for other individuals and investors. Understanding what's involved in real estate fix-up can make you millions on deals others pass up or allow you to build a profitable business providing these services to others.

When I started investing in real estate, I knew virtually nothing about doing repairs and renovations, but I learned. I figured out what

I could do myself, what I had to hire others to do (such as plumbing, electrical work, and roofing), and how to estimate the costs of everything. It's been years since I've picked up a paintbrush, but that foundation of knowledge continues to serve me well, even with my major commercial projects.

*Don't fall in love with your investment property.*

When it comes to rehabbing, the best advice I can offer is this: Don't fall in love with your investment property. This isn't your home, so don't treat it that way. Make quality repairs and renovations, but don't spend any more money than you have to. For example, you may love the look of wallpaper and have it in most of the rooms of your own home, but for your investment properties, paint is sufficient. Or you may like bright, dramatic colors on your walls, but the colors in your investment properties should be neutral so they will blend with any furnishings.

You can function as the general contractor on all your rehab projects and for other property owners. Typically, general contractors don't do any of the work; they manage the project by doing the estimates, hiring and supervising the subcontractors, and generally overseeing the job until it is completed satisfactorily. You do not need a license to function as a general contractor on property you own. If you are going to start a business as a general contractor working for others, you may need certain professional licenses and permits; check with your state's department of professional regulation or business to find out what's required.

Always take before-and-after photographs of every property you rehab for your files. Create a portfolio to show to lenders, other investors, and even sellers to demonstrate what you can do.

## Land Development

Once you have some experience with these proven real estate investment strategies, you may want to get into the development business, buying raw land and turning it into homes, apartments, offices, retail stores, and so on. I'll tell you exactly how to do that in Chapters 14 and 15.

## Part- or Full-Time

Another huge attraction of real estate investing is that you can do it part- or full-time. I've already told you that you should be passionate about how you're spending your time. If you're passionate about real estate, great—spend your time on your real estate business. But if you'd rather be doing something else, fine. Do real estate part-time to build your financial security, and do what you love—which may not be quite as lucrative—the rest of the time. Real estate investing doesn't have to distract you from your passion. Rather, it's a way to support your passion and free you up so you can do what you really want to.

## Why I Teach Investing

I make a lot more money investing in real estate than I do in the education business. I could shut down the education company tomorrow and I would probably become wealthier than I would with my education company because I'd have more time to focus on real estate.

The education business is something that captured my heart and soul a long time ago. I have always enjoyed sharing the wealth of knowledge that I have with others. I am a product of this industry, so I know it works. I love being in the classroom, teaching people how to invest and how to make their time worth more, and seeing the look in their eyes when they get it. I love training the investors who train for us, teaching them how to effectively share their knowledge and wisdom with our students. I love the letters and e-mails I get from people who tell me that what we taught them changed their lives. And I love knowing that I am helping people.

Does the education business make money? Yes, it does. I'm not going to apologize for that. Did I have a dream of building it into an international operation that helps people all over the world? Yes, I did. And that dream has come true.

I'm also not going to apologize for encouraging you to invest in your education. I believe the Whitney Education Group offers the absolute best financial training in the world, so naturally I think you should get at least some of your education from us. I also think you need to gain knowledge from other sources—read books by a variety of different authors, take classes on various subjects from any reliable source you can find. Our employees routinely attend seminars on a wide range of business issues. The company pays for it, and they come back full of ideas to build our organization and make it better for our students.

The Bible tells us to use our gifts to serve others and glorify God. The apostle Peter wrote, "Each one should use whatever gift he has received to serve others, faithfully administering God's grace in its various forms. If anyone speaks, he should do it as one speaking the very words of God. If anyone serves, he should do it with the strength God provides, so that in all things God may be praised through Jesus Christ."

I believe I have been given the gift of speaking and teaching. Because God has entrusted me with this gift, I feel I must use it to help others and, through that effort, serve God.

Now you have an idea of what you can do in real estate, and you understand my motivation for sharing what I know. Next, let's take a look at what might get in your way as you begin developing your millionaire mindset.

▼

# CHAPTER 3

# What's Stopping You?

If you believe investing in real estate is a good way to build wealth—and I'm sure you do because you're reading this book—what's stopping you? Chances are, it's a lack of belief in yourself, a lack of knowledge, and/or a lack of confidence. And those circumstances create fears that can paralyze you.

Let's take a look at the specific fears that stop people from fulfilling their dreams and how you can overcome them.

## Fear of Failure

Probably the most common reason people don't try new things is the fear of failure. They're afraid they'll fail—that they'll lose money—and everyone will laugh at them.

When my wife and I were getting ready to buy our first investment property, we were scared to death. I had read a book and then explained the ideas and strategies for investing to her. We thought it all made sense, but when it came to actually making that first real estate purchase, we were terrified.

It didn't help that people we trusted were planting negative seeds in our minds. For example, I remember talking about real estate investing with my father-in-law, a great guy, a wonderful family man, responsible, with a strong work ethic. And when he gave me advice, he was only trying to help and protect me. So when I told him we were planning to buy a duplex, fix it up, and rent it out, he focused on everything that could go wrong. What would I do if all the tenants moved out? What if the roof needed replacing? Or if the plumbing went bad? What about all those middle-of-the-night phone calls from tenants with problems?

As a result, my wife and I were afraid not only that the deal might not work but, if it didn't, that all the people who told us not to do it would say, "I told you so."

We were so afraid of failing and of being laughed at that we almost scared ourselves out of doing it.

But then we looked at everything rationally. We figured that people have been renting homes in this country for more than 200 years. People have been investing in real estate in this country for more than 200 years. Would all of the tenants move out, all the roofs start leaking, all the plumbing back up just because *we* bought an investment property? Of course not.

We had also done our homework on the property we wanted to buy. We knew what the units would rent for. We knew what our costs (mortgage, taxes, insurance, water, sewer, maintenance, vacancy allowance, etc.) would be. And we knew that the property would generate positive cash flow. It wasn't a gamble; it was a calculated investment.

At the time, my wife and I were both working at the slaughterhouse where we met. We had what were considered decent, reasonably secure jobs. In fact, when I got that job, I thought it was the best job I'd ever have. But I wanted more. And I remember looking at my wife and saying, "You know what, I'm scared to death and I know you are, too. But if we don't do this, if we don't take a shot here, we'll never have a chance at doing any better than our $5- and $6-an-hour jobs."

So we did it. And it worked. And we thought we'd never have to face the fear of failure again, and we didn't.

Until our second deal.

Actually, I think we were more afraid of doing our second and third deals than we were of the first. The first deal had worked—what if it was a fluke? What if the next deal didn't work and wiped out everything we made on the first one? Also, we were afraid we were getting greedy because we still wanted more.

We managed to overcome our fears and do those second and third deals, and they worked. And we started feeling fairly confident. We thought we'd never have to face the fear of failure again. And we didn't, as long as we were doing small deals. But then we ran across our first $500,000 deal, and all those feelings, all those doubts and fears, came rushing back because we were doing something we'd never done before, and we were afraid.

*Don't let your fears scare you into inaction.*

We were able to recognize our feelings and understand where they were coming from. We faced our fears with logic and reason. We educated ourselves about what we were doing; we knew the numbers were right, and we were prepared for contingencies, so we did the deal and it worked.

And we didn't have to face the fear of failure again—until we did our first $1 million deal.

If you are not investing in real estate because you are afraid you'll fail, your feelings are very normal. A lot of people feel this way. The key is to not let your fears scare you into inaction, but use them to prepare yourself well enough so that you won't fail.

One way to deal with the fear of failure is to consider the absolute worst-case scenario and figure out what you would do if that happened. If you know you can deal with the worst that can happen, you have no reason to be afraid.

*The best and easiest way to deal with the fear of failure is to build your confidence with knowledge.*

Raul is a student of mine who began investing at the age of twenty in California. When he and his brother took their initial training, Raul was both skeptical and afraid. He had been going to college and working during the summer, and he didn't want to lose the money he'd saved.

"But my brother said, 'You know, we are young enough that we can make a mistake and be able to come back and be okay,'" Raul told me.

It turned out that he didn't make a mistake. But if he had, he would have been able to recover, because he considered the worst-case scenario and made a calculated investment.

The best and easiest way to deal with the fear of failure is to build your confidence with knowledge. Learn about investing in real estate. Understand the formulas so you can determine the potential of a property. Become familiar with the language so you can talk with lenders, other investors, Realtors, and so on, without being intimidated. As you gain knowledge and confidence, you'll get excited and enthusiastic—and when that happens, it's easy to overcome the fear of failure.

## Fear of Ridicule

I see fear of ridicule among my students all the time—they're not just afraid of being ridiculed for failing, they're afraid of being ridiculed for even trying.

You can't do much about what other people say, but you *can* control how you react to it. People who ridicule others for trying to achieve their dreams have lost hope in their own ability to do the same. The only way they know how to build themselves up is by putting someone else down. It's sad—but it's not your problem.

Remember this: No one ever died from embarrassment. Don't let the fear of ridicule stop you. Instead, tune out the critics and focus on what you want to accomplish. It won't be long before looking at your bank balance will take care of any ridicule you might be the target of.

Believe me, you are not the only person who has ever been afraid of being ridiculed. And that's why I also say this: Don't ever laugh at anyone else's dreams. Dreams are important, and people who don't have dreams don't have much. If you didn't have dreams, you wouldn't be reading this book. You don't want your dreams ridiculed; so don't ridicule anyone else's.

## Fear of Success

The fear of success can be almost as paralyzing as the fear of failure—and it often follows when you've conquered the fear of failure. It's a bit ironic that you work so hard to overcome being afraid that you'll fail, then you achieve some success, and all of a sudden you're afraid that you won't be able to sustain your success.

For me, that point came when we had our first thirty or forty units. Things were going well, the rents were coming in, the properties were throwing off positive cash flow, we were paying our expenses—everything was happening as it was supposed to. But we had grown our real estate investments fairly quickly, and I started to worry that maybe we'd gotten in over our heads. There was absolutely no logical reason for that fear, but it crippled me. I actually stopped buying real estate for almost a year because I was afraid of the success. Had I not done that, we would have reached our financial goals much faster, but I needed to take some time to grow into my success.

Most real estate investors don't rush out and buy a 100- or 200-unit building for their first purchase. They start with a single-family house or a duplex, and then another, and another, and gradually move into larger buildings and bigger deals. It's a process that takes time, and that's good, because it gives you time to grow into it and get comfortable with what you're doing.

What happened to me was that I started out just a little bit too fast and my fears caught up with me. I had to slow down and get comfortable with what I was doing, and believe that it had worked and would continue to work as long as I did things right. Essentially, I had to learn to trust myself and believe that I was making my dreams come true.

Some people let the fear of success sabotage their efforts. They're afraid of what might happen when they become successful, so they deliberately do things that will keep them from being successful. They might drop out of school when they're just a few credits shy of graduation, or they might be up for a promotion at work and start coming in late and end up getting fired. In the case of a real estate investor, someone who is self-sabotaging might buy a property when the numbers clearly don't work and they know it. Or they'll rent to a tenant who has a history of being evicted for nonpayment. They do things like that so they don't have to deal with being successful.

I also think some people use the fear of success as an excuse. They say things like "I'd like to invest in real estate, but I don't want the lifestyle of Donald Trump" or "I don't want to have to worry that people will try to take advantage of me for my money."

You can be wealthy and not live in the spotlight that Trump does. Sam Walton built the biggest retail empire on the planet and still lived very modestly. You don't have to let anyone take advantage of you—whether it's for your time, your emotions, or your money.

When success comes, it can be a little frightening. Recognize that and put together a plan that will allow you to grow personally as your assets grow.

## Fear That You're Not Worthy of Wealth

Too many people never take action to become wealthy because they feel that they don't deserve it. The root of this is typically found in one's childhood programming—all those negative things, some well-meaning and some not, that people have said all your life.

*Don't get greedy.*

*People like us don't get rich.*

*What makes you think you can do that when so many others have failed?*

*Be realistic—just get a job.*

*This is the way it is in our world; you need to accept that and live with it.*

Messages such as these will block the development of a million-aire mindset.

Greed is defined as the excessive desire to acquire or possess more than one needs or deserves. I admit that I have many things I don't need; I have them because I want them, enjoy them, and can afford them. But I feel I deserve everything I have, because I've earned it.

A high-school dropout from a working-class background who once got into serious trouble, I could have easily bought into the message that I wasn't worthy of achieving anything significant in

*I am worthy of wealth and so are you.*

my life. But I realized that the people who said those kinds of things were wrong. The fact is, I *am* worthy of wealth and so are *you*. Believing that is a key part of the millionaire mindset.

## Fear of Not Being Able to Find Deals

The fear of failure and the fear of success are the two principal reasons people do not reach their financial goals. Other excuses for not becoming a real estate millionaire are just that: excuses.

Some people are afraid they won't be able to find deals. That's a fear that's difficult for me to understand. How to find deals is covered in the training Whitney Education Group provides, and in almost every real estate book on the market. Admittedly, it is much easier to find deals after you have a few under your belt and you can start earning referrals. All that means is that finding your first few deals may be a bit more challenging. But it is eminently possible and even probable.

Think about this: Let's say you're thinking about buying a convenience store franchise. Do you worry that you'll run a sale to attract customers and no one will come in?

Or let's say you've always wanted to be a hairstylist. Do you not go to school to earn your license because you're afraid that you won't be able to find anyone who needs a haircut?

The fact is, if you have a convenience store and you keep it clean and well-stocked, you price your products competitively, and you follow a well-thought-out marketing plan, you'll have customers. If you become a hairstylist and can listen to people and cut their hair the way they want, you'll have customers. It's the same thing with real estate: If you learn how to do it, you'll be able to find deals.

To be successful as a real estate investor, you need to be able to find people who have a problem that can be solved with the sale, purchase, or rental of real estate. The problem doesn't necessarily have to be catastrophic, it just has to be a problem that you can help solve. Do you think that just because you decide to invest in real estate all the motivation for selling property will disappear? That all the tenants will disappear?

Of course not. There will never be a shortage of people wanting to buy, sell, or rent real estate. And that means there will never be a shortage of potential deals—regardless of what is motivating the buyer or seller, or regardless of why a potential tenant is looking for a place to live.

## Fear of Not Having the Money to Do Deals

The fear of not having money to fund a deal is another groundless fear. I didn't have any money when I started. Nor did most of our trainers. In fact, most of our students start with little or no money of their own and go on to build impressive real estate portfolios.

If the fear of not having money is what's holding you back, here's the good news: There is plenty of money out there, and there are plenty of ways for you to finance real estate deals. You just need to know how to do it. I'll discuss that in more detail in Chapters 17 and 18.

## Getting Started

Now you know the causes of what might be stopping you. And by understanding that, you can deal with it. So now let's get started.

# CHAPTER 4

# The Power of Positive Thinking Combined with Effort

I am a big believer in the power of positive thinking. It is an absolutely integral part of the millionaire mindset. But while negative thinking can stop you from reaching your goals, positive thinking alone won't get you there. You must do the work.

Helen Keller once wrote, "The world is sown with good; but unless I turn my glad thoughts into practical living and till my own field, I cannot reap a kernel of the good." You need to till your field, and you need to do it with a great attitude. When positive thinking is combined with hard work, you are virtually unstoppable.

## Break Free from Your Old Programming

The most common reason for failing to achieve success is self-imposed limitations. If you believe you can't do any better than holding down a job for a middle-income paycheck, then you won't.

So many people believe that because that's how they've been raised and programmed from birth. All of the adults they trust— parents, grandparents, siblings, aunts, uncles, teachers, pastors— have been sending them messages:

*Play it safe.*

*Go to school.*

*Get a good job.*

*Don't take risks.*

*Be content with mediocrity.*

This is powerful programming, and it's not easy to overcome. But it can be done. I know, because I did it, and I've taught my students how to do it.

You know that the financial side of real estate is, for the most part, just eighth-grade math. Think about it: Add up the income (rents), subtract the expenses, and if you have money left over, that's positive cash flow, and it's a good thing. Take the amount of positive cash flow, divide it into your down payment, and you get the rate of return on your money. It really is that simple. But if you're going to do it, you have to believe it.

*The financial side of real estate is, for the most part, just eighth-grade math.*

If you're going to develop the millionaire mindset, you need to start by believing that it's possible for you to become a millionaire and removing the mental limits that have held you back so far. Who is in charge of your life? Is it the naysayers who shoot down your dreams? Or is it you?

If you're going to be wealthy and successful, you need to be listening to people who are wealthy and successful, people who are positive, people who will tell you it can be done and you can do it. You need to believe them, and take charge of your life so you can do what needs to be done to reach your goals. Mark Twain said,

"Keep away from people who try to belittle your ambitions. Small people always do that, but the really great make you feel that you, too, can become great."

Trust me on this: You can do it!

The simplest and most effective way to change your old negative programming is to first recognize that you have it and then make a conscious decision to change it. If you have a negative mindset, it's probably because of what's been fed you your whole life by people you care about, trust, and respect—your parents, teachers, preachers, and so on—as well as by mass-media messages. People aren't born with negative or positive attitudes; they develop them by what they are taught.

*Basic time and resource management is something wealthy people do intuitively.*

You can begin to change your attitude when you start to replace negativity with as much positive material from as many different excellent sources as you can. I believe that if you fill up your mind with good information, there won't be room for any negative thoughts or beliefs.

If you doubt that repeating affirmations works, think about the advertising industry. Companies spend millions of dollars to send the same message, over and over, in an effort to persuade you to buy their products. You can "just do it" in Nike shoes. You can "reach out and touch someone" with AT&T. "Let your fingers do the walking" through the Yellow Pages and know that "you're worth it" when it comes to the price of L'Oréal hair products. And your Visa credit card is "everywhere you want to be."

If these slogans sound familiar, it's because positive repetition works. I heard a story once about a Chinese girl who moved to the United States. She wanted an English name and chose the name Patience so that she would be reminded to be patient every time she heard someone say her name. When a college professor shared that story with her students and asked what names they would select for themselves, one young man's response was: "Rich."

I'm not suggesting that you change your name. But I am suggesting that you use the technique of positive reinforcement. Make sure the things you see and hear are positive and will help you reach your goals.

Recognize that you have a choice. You are not destined to live with negative beliefs. You are not destined to be positive. You are who you are now because of what you have been taught. To fashion a different mindset is just a matter of retraining yourself.

I have seen so many people make the decision to become more positive, and the change is incredible. Even with a lifetime of negative programming, people make significant progress in just *a day*.

A word of caution: When you begin to "reprogram" yourself, you may experience some sadness about all the time you've wasted living in a world of negativity. Don't be sad. Don't waste time looking back at the past with regrets. Instead, learn from the past and look forward.

Once you begin regularly feeding your mind with positive, worthwhile information, you will find you are developing and sharpening your millionaire mindset. Soon you'll be ready to choose an aspect of real estate to begin building your fortune.

## Are You Procrastinating?

Do you make it a habit of putting things off until the last minute? Or do you not ever get to them at all? Are you thinking about the techniques you've learned in this book and telling yourself, "This sounds like it will work for me, and I'll do it—just as soon as I . . ." and then fill in whatever excuse comes to mind? In my book, you can either be good at making excuses, or you can be good at making money. But you can't do both.

I'm not saying that those who procrastinate are lazy; I'm sure some are, but most are not. What I see more is the fear behind procrastination—usually the fears of failure and success that I talked about in Chapter 3.

Let's walk through the process. What is your overall goal? Be specific. Don't say, "I want to be rich." Instead, make your goal very measurable. For example: "One year from now, I want to own twenty rental units that generate $30,000 a year in positive cash flow; hold four properties under lease options; and create $30,000 in cash from assigning contracts."

Take these goals and break them down. To own twenty rental units means you have to average buying almost two single-family houses a month or a fourplex every two and a half months. To get four properties under lease options (which you'll learn how to do in Chapter 12) means you have to do one deal per quarter. If you average $5,000 for each contract you assign (the technique is explained in Chapter 11), you need to do one every other month.

Now, what do you have to do to accomplish these very realistic goals? Make a list: Build your Power Team (which I'll explain in Chapter 8); put together and implement a marketing plan; join your local real estate investors club; read books and take courses that will give you the education you need. Create a "to do" list and prioritize each task. Be realistic; don't give yourself thirty hours of top-priority tasks to do in Week One. Figure out what's important and what needs to be done first, and then start checking things off your list.

If you're not getting things done, ask yourself why—and don't accept excuses. This is a private exercise, so don't worry about what other people think. If your task for the day was to order your "I Buy Real Estate" signs but you didn't get it done, be honest with

yourself about why not. If you can't come up with the right word-
ing, or if you're not sure you're getting the best price, or if you
can't decide on the colors, what's probably really going on is that
you're masking your fears. Are you afraid that you're going to buy
the signs, put them out, and then no one will call? Or worse, someone will call and you'll have to talk to him? Get to the root of
what's really driving your behavior.

Focus on getting one task done at a time. If you start something,
jump to something else, then go to still something else, you'll
never finish anything—but you'll be exhausted at the end of the
day. Get one task done, check it off your list, and move on to the
next.

Recognize that you're changing habits that have taken a lifetime
to develop, so if you have an off day, that's okay. Recognize it for
what it is, and get back on track tomorrow.

## Focus on the Positive

Do you know anyone who has selective hearing? If you have kids,
you probably do. They're great at hearing what they want ("Sure,
you can go to that party") and not hearing what they don't want
("if you clean your room first"). My dogs are the same way. They
never miss "Do you want a treat?," but they often go conveniently
deaf when the command is "Sit, stay."

I recommend that you, too, develop selective hearing—but from
the perspective that you learn to tune out negativity. There are
people in this world who just love to find the bad in things, who
love to seek out the negative. And worse, negative people love to
encourage other people to be negative—they love to bring other
people down. I shun negativity, and I surround myself with positive people. You should do the same.

Here's a great story to illustrate the value of this practice:

A bunch of tiny frogs arranged a race. The goal was to see which one could reach the top of a very high tower first. A big crowd gathered around the tower to watch the race and cheer on the contestants. But no one really believed that any of the tiny frogs could reach the top of the tower. The people in the crowd were shouting things like "Oh, this is way too difficult!" and "They'll *never* make it to the top!" and "They don't have a chance to succeed. The tower is too high."

One by one, the tiny frogs began giving up. Still, some continued climbing, and the crowd continued yelling, "It's too difficult. They can't do this!" And more and more of the tiny frogs gave up.

But one continued going higher and higher. This one frog wouldn't give up. At the end of the race, after all of the other frogs had quit, this one tiny frog had reached the top of the tower.

One of the frogs that had quit asked the frog that had succeeded how he had found the strength to reach his goal. But the winning frog couldn't hear him. It turned out that the winning frog was deaf—he couldn't hear any of the negative things the spectators had been saying.

*Turn a deaf ear to anyone who tries to tell you that you cannot achieve your dreams.*

This story makes two very important points. First, never listen to other people when they are being negative or pessimistic. Second, never underestimate the power of words.

So turn a deaf ear to anyone who tries to tell you that you cannot achieve your dreams. More important, listen to the people who believe in you and who want to help you succeed.

Writer Po Bronson put it very well when he said, "There's a powerful transformative effect when you surround yourself with like-minded people. Peer pressure is a great thing when it helps you accomplish your goals instead of distracting you from them."

When other people say negative things, it usually reflects their own fears. You can be sympathetic to it, but don't expose yourself to it. More to the point—don't accept their fears. You probably already have plenty of your own that you're working on overcoming.

## Can *You* Really Do This?

Not long ago in one of our advanced classes, students were introducing themselves and telling why they had gotten into real estate. One young couple had a two-year-old child, and the woman was pregnant with twins. She saw how important real estate could be to their future. But in the beginning, her husband was reluctant. When he continued to resist making the investment in training, she told him, "You do this, or we're history." So he decided to do it. Of course, she was joking—I think. But she made her point.

In that same class, another couple recounted that they'd seen some testimonials from our students on television. And the woman said, "We can do this." And so they did.

You can build tremendous wealth investing in real estate—if you think positive and work hard.

## Turning Thoughts into Action

You've probably heard this from more than one place: To become a millionaire, you need to learn to think like a millionaire. That's true, but it's only the first step. Thinking like a rich person is important, but it's acting like a rich person that gets you results. When you think and act like a rich person, you have the millionaire mindset.

# CHAPTER 5

# When Things
# Go Wrong

I wish I could tell you that if you follow my advice, you'll never have another problem in your life. That's just not true.

Virtually every business comes with its own obstacles that need to be overcome, and real estate investing is no exception. You're going to have deals that fall through, you're going to have difficult tenants, you're going to have unexpected repairs—and stomping your feet, huffing and puffing, and complaining endlessly isn't going to solve anything.

It doesn't matter how big your bank account is—everyone in this world has problems. You must accept the fact that things will sometimes go wrong. What counts is not that you have to face hurdles, but how you deal with these situations. The late author and speaker Leo Buscaglia once said, "There are two big forces at work, external and internal. We have very little control over external forces such as tornadoes, earthquakes, floods, disasters, illness, and pain. What really matters is the internal force. How do I respond to those disasters? Over that I have complete control."

Don't look at problems as situations that will stop you from succeeding; see them as challenges that strengthen and enrich you when you solve them.

## Tell Your Side of the Story

Often what appears to be a huge problem is actually just something that can be dealt with through effective communication. When you're trying to accomplish something and people don't understand it, they're going to object to it. That's human nature.

Not long ago, I applied to have a piece of property rezoned from residential to mixed use. At the first public hearing (which is standard procedure for a rezoning request), everybody from the adjacent neighborhoods showed up to protest. Okay, maybe it wasn't *everybody*, but there were a lot of people who apparently thought that we wanted to build some kind of heavy industrial center. That wasn't what we wanted to do at all. So for the second public hearing, I had an architect create a rendering that would show people exactly what we had planned, which was an attractive mixed-use center that would make shopping easier for the nearby residents and provide other benefits.

*View problems as challenges that strengthen and enrich you when you solve them.*

Instead of letting them use their own imagination and visualize smokestacks and manufacturing plants and traffic congestion, I showed them precisely what I intended to do. They saw the benefits and withdrew their opposition to the rezoning. Instead of having to do battle with a frightened band of opponents, I now had a substantial group of supporters—because I told my side of the story clearly and honestly.

## Recognize Real Estate and
## Economic Cycles

It doesn't take an in-depth study of history to recognize that life and business are a series of cycles. Some are easier to predict than others, but they are cycles nonetheless. Even the Bible speaks of this in a well-known passage from Ecclesiastes: "There is a time for everything, and a season for every activity under heaven." The

*The economy and real estate go through cycles that are fairly easy to recognize.*

point: There are cycles to life that we need to understand, accept, and learn how to function within. Business cycles are not as predictable as the seasons, but you can count on them happening.

The economy and real estate go through cycles that are fairly easy to recognize. But whether the cycle is up or down doesn't matter—there are always opportunities. The key is to know how to recognize them and take advantage of them. Even when the economy is down, business doesn't stop. People may cut back on extras, but they still need food, clothing, shelter, transportation, and medical care.

Keep in mind, too, that cycles can be local and regional, as well as national and even global. They are also segmented by industry. It seems to be the job of the news media to present whatever is happening in the worst possible light. Don't buy into their negativity. Look beyond the headlines, understand what is really going on, and figure out how to work with the circumstances.

Can economic cycles hurt you? It's possible. That's why you need to pay attention and prepare for them. The U.S. economy is like the *Titanic*—it's huge, and it changes direction slowly. You'll have time to watch trends, evaluate them, and adjust your own strategies accordingly.

Sometimes you'll take swift, decisive action in response to a business cycle; other times, you may choose to sit back and ride things out. If you are investing wisely and according to the methods I teach, you'll have the resources to survive a downturn—and even prosper greatly during such a cycle—as well as the knowledge to capitalize on the upturns.

## Do What Is Proven to Work

Recently, one of my students came to me for advice. She was in a serious cash crunch—her negative cash flow was more than $10,000 a month. I knew she understood the methods I teach, and at first I couldn't figure out how she got herself into this situation. Then the truth came out: She was living beyond her means (instead of below them, as I recommend); she had gotten too friendly with many of her tenants, and they were taking advantage of her; she was spending more than she needed to on repairs and renovations; and she had purchased a number of nonperforming properties (properties that were not generating revenue) without an exit plan and had become emotionally attached to them.

*When successful people tell you what **not** to do, listen to them.*

If she had stuck to the proven plan we teach, she would have been generating plenty of positive cash flow and could have afforded the luxuries she wanted for her family. But she let herself get off track. Fortunately, she had the good sense to let one of our student counselors help her work out a plan to get back on track.

I'm not saying you shouldn't try new things. But the foundation of your real estate investing should be based on techniques that have been proven to work. When successful people tell you what *not* to do, listen to them. Learn from their mistakes, and you'll have fewer problems of your own to deal with.

## Learn from Your Failures

It's great when you can learn from other people's failures, but that won't completely stop you from having at least a few of your own. Always take the time to learn from your failures. Figure out what happened, what went wrong, and what you can do to prevent it from happening again.

## People Don't Always Do What They Say

It's just a fact of human nature: People don't always do what they say they will. Sometimes broken promises are accidental, some- times intentional—in business, that doesn't really matter. What matters is that when someone doesn't follow through on a commit- ment, you have to deal with the consequences.

Regardless of how well you know someone, when you're in a business deal, you need the terms and conditions written down, and everyone involved needs to sign off on the details.

Written agreements are the greatest way to protect your busi- ness relationships. When you talk through the details, then put them all down on paper; everyone involved has the chance to say, "Wait a minute, that's not what I thought we were agreeing to" before the contract is signed. And if you can't settle on terms that everyone is happy with, you don't do the deal—and nobody feels like they weren't treated fairly.

I have heard people carry on nostalgically about a time when "a man's word was his bond" and you could "do a deal on a handshake." When I give my word, I keep it. You should, too. But still put together a written agreement.

Contracts let everybody involved see what the deal is, clearly, in writing. It's a chance for you to say, "Yes, I agree with this." It's also a chance for you to say, "No, this isn't what I thought we were going to do." And you work out the details before you have a huge problem. This is especially important when you're putting together large development deals.

When your agreement is written down and everybody signs it, there's no room for anyone to say later that the deal is not as he understood. And people will do that: It's not that they're trying to be dishonest, it's that they either truly don't remember the details or they genuinely misunderstood.

Never draw up a contract that isn't fair to everyone—and never sign a contract that puts you at a disadvantage. Most important: Never sign a contract you haven't read and completely understood. When you sign a contract, you're going to be held to its terms, whether or not you know what they are, and whether or not you understand them.

## Critical Contract Clauses

Of course, even with the best of written agreements, there will be times when someone doesn't hold up their end of the deal, so every contract also needs to have a nonperformance clause. Essentially, this is the clause that says, "Here's what's going to happen if any party to this contract doesn't meet the terms of the contract."

Here is an example of why that's so important. I was involved in a joint venture with a guy who didn't come up with his share of the money. It was a complicated real estate deal that involved multiple closings and was worth about a $4 million profit. At the first closing, this guy didn't have his share of the money (which was about $300,000), so I signed a note to get him through. At the second closing, he didn't have the money again—not the initial amount, or the second round of funding. I was willing to make allowances the first time, but not the second time. My reputation was on the line. Our agreement allowed me to put in his share of the money—and take his share of the profit. And that's what I did.

*Always think positive—and always be prepared for things to go wrong.*

In any deal where you are working with one or more partners who are required to put up money at specified times, you need contractual remedies to deal with anyone who defaults on their commitment. Those remedies need to include strong financial penalties and allow the partner or partners who are meeting their obligations to take control of the project. And the remedies should be mutual—you should face the same penalties that everyone else involved does. Nobody gets a free pass.

I never get into a deal if there is any doubt that I'll be able to fulfill the terms of the contract. People know that about me, they know they can trust me, and that's why I never have any trouble putting together profitable deals and attracting investors. Build that kind of reputation for yourself, and you'll never have a shortage of opportunities for making money. It really boils down to this: Don't make promises unless you're sure you can keep them.

Nonperformance clauses are also very common in construction. Essentially, you set a deadline and have penalties in place if the deadline isn't met. I also recommend that you include a reward clause—if the job gets done early or even on time, there's a bonus or reward involved.

There are some other clauses that I routinely include in all my contracts. One addresses cause—that is, it outlines that you can be released from the contract for cause and defines what that is. For example, if someone commits fraud or does something illegal, you are not obligated to the terms of the contract.

I also include something I call a dual-venue clause. Many attorneys have begun using this clause in their other contracts after I've given it to them. Essentially, it addresses the issue of venue in the case of litigation. Most people want to have the venue be where they are. That means that if I enter into a contract with someone in Oregon and he has venue, and there is litigation, I have to travel from Florida across the country to deal with it.

My venue terms are these: If we have a contract and I sue you, I have to come to where you are. If you sue me, you have to come to Florida. It's fair, it's a great deterrent to litigation, and it really encourages people to try a little harder to work out any conflicts before they end up in court.

## Always Be Prepared for the Unthinkable

As I've said before, I am a big believer in positive thinking. The mind is an incredibly powerful tool; when it is nourished with positive messages, it can produce phenomenal results. I figured this out early in my real estate investing career, and it's been an integral part of everything I teach ever since.

There is a difference between positive thinking and ignoring reality. No amount of positive thinking could have stopped the hurricanes that devastated Florida in 2004. No amount of positive thinking can stop any natural disaster, including earthquakes, tornadoes, and blizzards. No amount of positive thinking can prevent fires, floods, burglaries, vandalism, and unexpected violence. What positive thinking *can* do is keep you on the right track while you're dealing with disasters.

The Bible tells us that God uses disasters to strengthen our character, to help us grow spiritually, and to bring us closer to Him. My point in mentioning this is to stress that good can come out of bad, and when we have to face adversity and challenge, we have the opportunity to become better people—and to build stronger businesses.

That's why, in addition to developing and maintaining the habit of positive thinking, you must still prepare for the unthinkable. You do this with a thorough disaster plan.

I can think of many, many things I'd rather do than sit down and figure out what I might need to do in the event of a disaster. But when you are actively investing in real estate, when you have tenants and employees who depend on you, when you have buyers and sellers who are waiting for their deals to close, you need a plan that will allow you to quickly react and recover when a disaster occurs.

## Basic Elements of a Disaster Plan

Your disaster plan needs to be written down, with copies maintained in your office and in the personal possession of key people in your organization. It's not enough to just have some ideas in your head—even if you are a one-person operation.

The most critical element of a disaster plan is communications. Your plan should include current contact information of all employees (if you have them), along with critical outside resources, such as insurance companies, suppliers, independent contractors, consultants, and so on. Consider how your tenants and employees will be kept informed during and after a disaster.

You also need to establish a chain of command and clearly define who is responsible for what during an emergency. Be sure that each critical task is handled and that you're not wasting time duplicating efforts. For example, if you have a crew working on a property and there's a fire or someone needs emergency medical attention, you don't need a dozen different people calling 911—but you need to make sure that at least one person makes that call, and makes it promptly.

Your disaster plan should also include data protection. Critical papers (contracts, leases, rental applications, other tenant records, etc.) and other important materials should be stored in fire- and waterproof cabinets. Your electronic files should be backed up and stored off-site. We have our servers fully backed up and the data stored in another city. If your operation doesn't have that kind of resource, you can use a commercial online storage system that allows you to upload your files on a daily basis and recover them from any location.

*Don't give up on your dreams just because the road will occasionally be rocky.*

Be sure you have adequate and appropriate insurance, including business-interruption coverage (which includes rental-income coverage) that will replace business income lost due to a covered peril. Ask your insurance agent exactly what type of documentation is required for claims and keep a regularly updated file with necessary information about facilities, equipment, furnishings, supplies, and so forth.

It's a good idea to establish a relationship with a public adjuster before you have a claim, too. Public adjusters (as opposed to insurance company adjusters) work for the insured. They handle all the paperwork and other steps involved in filing a claim, and they make sure you get what you are due under the terms of your policy. This is an area of expertise that few businesses have in-house, and it's well worth the fee. Also, many insurance company adjusters would rather work with a public adjuster than the actual client, because the public adjuster isn't emotional about the loss. You can find public adjusters listed in your local telephone directory, or contact the National Association of Public Insurance Adjusters (NAPIA) at www.napia.com.

# Tenants' Responsibility

As a property manager or landlord, it is unlikely that you'll be on-site when an emergency occurs. Your tenants need to understand what to do in the event of a disaster to protect their own lives and property and also to keep the damage to the building as minimal as possible.

Provide your tenants with written emergency response instructions as part of your rental agreement. Use this sample as a guide:

### Tenant Emergency Response Instructions

In the event of a situation or disaster that has the potential to injure people or damage property, the tenant has the responsibility to:

▼ Immediately call 911 for appropriate police, fire, or medical rescue assistance.

▼ If possible to accomplish safely, secure property to avoid additional damage. This includes turning off water and power as appropriate, covering damaged roofs with tarps, covering broken windows, and so on.

▼ Notify management of incident as soon as possible. [Include after-hours emergency notification procedures.]

▼ Provide copies of any official reports (police, fire, etc.) to management within three working days.

▼ Cooperate with management by providing access for insurance claims adjusters, repair estimators, and repair workers so the property damage may be evaluated and repaired as quickly as possible. Should there be any problems with this process, or if any estimators or workers fail to report on schedule, notify management so appropriate action can be taken.

## Litigation Is a Fact of Life

For many years, I took great pride in the fact that I had never been sued and that I had never sued anyone. I felt that if you were involved in a lawsuit, you were somehow tainted. And then my companies and my various business interests continued to grow— and somebody filed a lawsuit against us. And I realized that we are in an age where litigation is just a part of doing business. My pride in avoiding lawsuits was misplaced and a result of ignorance, and there was nothing inherently bad about me or my company because someone sued us.

It doesn't matter what you do—if you are in business, you're probably going to get sued at some point. In the United States, it's estimated that a new lawsuit is filed every thirty seconds. And as the value of your assets increases, so do the chances that you'll be sued. The suit may or may not have merit. It might be a disgruntled employee who left on bad terms and wants to "get even" with you; it might be a tenant who was physically injured on your property and wants compensation; or it might be an investor/partner who claims you didn't do something you agreed to. The list of potential causes of action for lawsuits is probably a lot longer than this book, and creative plaintiffs and their attorneys come up with new ones every day. And then there's the fact that some people try to use legal sources improperly—those cases are usually tossed out, but you still have to deal with them.

You can't afford to ignore the potential of either being the target of litigation or being in a situation where you need to initiate a lawsuit.

## When You Get Sued

Lawsuits rarely come as a surprise. Depending on the situation, you will likely have had some degree of informal discussion with the other party and have been unable to reach an agreement. Most attorneys will try to resolve the dispute through various types of negotiations before actually filing suit. It is extremely unlikely that you'll ever be served with a lawsuit you knew nothing about ahead of time.

Even so, you might panic the day the process server arrives. Relax. You will always have a reasonable amount of time to respond to the suit—you don't have to do it the same day you're served.

If you don't already have an attorney, get one. I generally like to use larger firms, because they have more resources and clout. The attorney handling your case should be someone you're comfortable with, a person you feel you can talk to and who listens to you. Remember that you're in charge. The attorney should explain the law, make sure you understand your various options, and even make a recommendation for a course of action—but the final decision is yours.

Whether or not your first reaction is panic, it's likely that you'll feel both indignant and angry about being sued. You may be tempted to write a scathing response to the plaintiff and his attorney. Go ahead and write the response. Vent all you want. Get everything out of your system. Then cull it down, take out the pure emotion, and send it to *your* attorney. The process can give your lawyer some valuable background and information and help you deal with your feelings at the same time.

Most lawsuits are settled before trial, and that is often the most prudent business strategy. In my own operations, we don't litigate unless we have to. Legal bills can add up very quickly, and it will often cost you less to settle than to go to court—even if you win. In those situations, the best business decision may be to settle, and you always want to handle a lawsuit in a manner that will deliver the best outcome for your business. For example, the plaintiff may be asking for $3,000 for what you think is a false slip-and-fall claim. As part of the pretrial process, you go through three or four rounds of depositions and attorneys for both sides make a few pre-trial motions, and before you know it, you've racked up $20,000 in expenses. It might make more sense to just pay the $3,000 and be done with it—even if you don't feel the claim is justified. Or, if you're sure you can prove it's a false claim and you want to avoid getting a reputation as someone who settles easily, you may decide to fight the claim because you believe it will be best in the long term. Make these decisions based on logic and reason, not emotion.

## When Should You Sue?

The other side of getting sued is doing the suing. Filing a lawsuit is a serious step—don't take it lightly. When I have a dispute with someone, I do everything possible to resolve the situation without going to court. That includes making phone calls, writing letters, and having my attorney write letters. Those initial efforts are always calm and reasonable—don't rant and rave, or threaten dire consequences. The message you want to communicate is "We have a problem here. Now how can we square it up and get it right?"

In many cases, that's all it takes. But if phone calls, letters, and attorney's letters don't work, you need to decide if the issue is worth going to court over. Sit down with your attorney and consider what you stand to gain and what it could cost you. You may decide it's better to just walk away—or you may decide you need to pursue the case.

## You'll Always Have Problems

No matter how successful we are, or how much wealth we amass, we all have challenges in our business lives from time to time. Deals will fall apart. People you trusted may betray you. You'll be tested from more angles than you knew were possible. But, as Martin Luther King, Jr., said, "The ultimate measure of a man is not where he stands in moments of comfort and convenience, but where he stands at times of challenge and controversy."

Ask yourself this: Should you give up on doing whatever it's going to take to make your dreams of wealth come true just because there's a chance things might not be absolutely perfect all the time?

I hope you answered no—because that means you're on your way to having the millionaire mindset.

▼

# CHAPTER 6

# Take It to the Next Level

When I first started investing in real estate, I had no idea I would end up where I am today. I was just looking for a way to build a financial future for myself and my family. I didn't foresee eventually becoming an owner or part owner of dozens of companies, including being the CEO of a publicly traded international training organization.

As you begin investing in real estate, you'll find that you, too, have many choices. You can be successful on a smaller scale, creating a comfortable living and achieving economic security for yourself and your family. Or you can move up to a higher level with a greater income. There's no right or wrong here; it all depends on what you want to do—and whether or not you have the millionaire mindset.

As successful as my early investments were, it didn't take me long to realize that, while I could build substantial wealth with real estate investing alone, creating some ancillary businesses and even diversifying beyond real estate would provide greater opportunity and security. For example, shortly after I bought my first few investment properties in New York, I created a contracting company to handle the rehab work and a management company to manage the properties.

Even though these were sole proprietorships that I personally owned and operated, setting up my business this way, rather than just doing everything as an individual investor, provided a variety of benefits. The separate entities made it easier to track my costs and profits, as well as identify various business patterns. As an individual, I had to pay full retail for rehab materials; my contracting company qualified for professional discounts, credit lines, and additional special services from paint stores, home-improvement stores, and other suppliers. Owning these companies also made it easier to borrow money for my investments. At the time, lenders were far more reluctant to approve loans for self-employed individuals than they are today. As an employee of a company—even one

*Create multiple streams of income so you are not totally dependent on any one source of revenue.*

that I owned—I was viewed as a better risk than I was as a self-employed independent investor. It was absurd, but I knew that if I wanted to borrow money, I had to play by the rules of the lenders.

While my initial purpose in creating these companies was to benefit my own investments, I quickly realized that I could provide services to other investors, and in the process create additional income for myself. And because that additional income came from sources other than my personal holdings, it provided me more financial diversity. As a wealth-building strategy, creating multiple streams of income— that is, not being totally dependent on any one source of revenue—is extremely important.

## The Lure of Sunshine and Greater Opportunity

Considering my age at the time and the fact that I had only a few years of experience, I had built a substantial portfolio of real estate investments in New York when I decided to investigate investing in Florida. From a business perspective, it made sense to look at areas that were growing and where property values were appreciating. From a personal perspective, I was tired of the cold and the snow and all the other aspects of dealing with upstate New York's harsh winters. So I sold my holdings, packed up my family, and we headed to southwest Florida.

The move turned out to be more of a learning experience than I had anticipated. But after a few initial obstacles, my real estate investment business was established and thriving. Although I was still reading and studying how-to books, I realized I had information to share that wasn't in any of the books on the market at the time. So I decided to write my own book, *Overcoming the Hurdles & Pitfalls of Real Estate Investing*. The manuscript was rejected by several major publishing houses before I struck a deal with a company to publish the book on the condition that I would go on the lecture circuit to promote it.

I was working hard, traveling around the country giving talks on real estate, and making a lot of money—but more important, I was helping people change their lives for the better. Because I wanted to be able to give people more in-depth information, I created my own training company. I also created my own publishing operation to produce my books, tapes, software, and eventually CDs and DVDs. These operations gave me the opportunity for some terrific on-the-job training in two new businesses.

I decided that if I could do this for myself, I could do it for others. So I found other bright people with worthwhile information to share and helped them set up training programs and put together support materials in the form of educational books, audio and video recordings, and live instruction. As the seminar and publishing businesses grew, it made sense to set up a mail-order operation and expand our sales.

As those companies thrived, I continued looking for additional opportunities. Intuitively, I understood the value of diversification. I had achieved my goal of becoming a millionaire at the age of twenty-seven, but I had no intention of stopping there. And it wasn't just because of the money—my businesses were making a difference in the lives of my customers. My tenants had safe, secure, sanitary housing. My students were learning how to invest in real estate and build their own financial futures. The trainers I worked with were helping other people and making a good living themselves. And my companies were providing jobs for people.

## How Should You Do It?

Most real estate investors start as I did, with low- and moderate-income units that they handle themselves. These are generally easier to buy, and they provide the best cash flow (compared to other residential rental property). But they are also the most management-intensive types of properties, and that can take its toll on you. After a while, many get tired of the work these properties require and look for investments that take less time and effort.

It seems to be a natural progression among the investors I know, especially the ones who have taken our training: They learn the business by buying the low- and moderate-income properties. After a period of time, they take their equity and start investing in nicer, easier-to-manage residential properties, and even commercial real estate.

As you go on in real estate investing, look for opportunities that will dovetail into your real estate business. Rehab and property-management companies are great examples—and when you're doing this kind of business, you are usually one of the first to know when a great property is going to be put on the market. You can either snag it for yourself or give an associate a heads-up about the deal.

*Learn the business with low- and moderate-income properties, then move up to nicer residential and even commercial real estate.*

You might want to get your real estate license so that you can pick up sales commissions on some of your transactions. As you gain experience, you might also get your mortgage broker's license.

This way, if you find several great pieces of real estate and you don't have the resources to buy them all, or some don't fit your particular investment strategy, instead of walking away with nothing from the listing, you can act as an agent and make a commission on the sale of the property. And as a mortgage broker, you can help the buyers line up financing and earn a commission there.

In addition to looking for business opportunities that are related to your real estate investing operation, be on the lookout for partnership opportunities. Don't try to do everything by yourself; there really is strength in numbers.

Shortly after I began buying raw land, I realized there was an opportunity in subdividing the land and building houses. I started by contracting with a builder, and it wasn't long before I was selling so many houses that the builder couldn't keep up. He was a terrific builder, but he needed help with the other aspects of his business. Instead of just bringing in another builder and splitting my business between the two, I suggested that the builder and I create a construction company. We brought in two more partners and made sure we had all our bases covered: operations, management, marketing, and sales. The four of us each have a percentage of ownership in the company. Currently, we're building more than 350 houses a year—and growing. We probably would have completed more houses last year if we hadn't had to deal with unprecedented material and labor shortages caused by the high demand for building supplies in China and the damage to Florida from four hurricanes in 2004. Our company is generating millions of dollars a year in revenue.

While the builder went from being a 100 percent owner of his company to being a part owner of the construction company we put together, he's making far more money. When he was running his own show, the best he could manage to do was to build about forty houses a year, and he was running himself ragged. With our

*Don't try to do everything by yourself; there is strength in numbers.*

partnership, he's not working as hard, he's much less stressed, and he's getting a handsome share of the profits from a company that's building hundreds of houses a year. What's more, our company is operating with greater efficiency. He is making ten times more than he made in business by himself and is enjoying life more.

Now, I personally don't know how to build a house. Sure, I understand the general process, but I don't know how to mix and pour the foundation, how to put up the walls and install the roof trusses, or how to install electrical wiring or plumbing. But not knowing how to build a house has not stopped me from building a highly profitable construction company, because I do understand the concept of how to buy a piece of vacant land and end up with a house a few months later.

In addition to the construction company, I also own a real estate development company; a mortgage company; a syndication company that puts together deals for investors to purchase acreage and other types of real estate; an interest in a title company; several small corporations that buy, sell, and develop real estate both domestically and internationally; and a number of other businesses.

These are all the kinds of businesses that you, too, can create and build. The experience you'll gain as a real estate investor can serve as your foundation, as you take your knowledge and skills in creating ancillary businesses to the next level. You just need to be sure you approach each opportunity with your eyes wide open, perform your due diligence, and put together a thorough plan. In doing so, you'll create win-win situations for you and your associates.

# CHAPTER 7

# Great Communications

Most successful businesspeople are excellent communicators. They may not necessarily be fabulous orators, but they know how to get their point across effectively and efficiently.

Good communication skills will do more than make it easier for you to be successful in real estate—they will enhance every aspect of your life, from your relationships with your spouse and kids to talking with employees, customers, clients, and others.

People are not born knowing how to communicate. It's a skill anyone can learn.

## Learn How to Listen

You have two ears and one mouth. Use them in proportion to those numbers, and you will automatically improve your communication skills. The late screenwriter Wilson Mizner once observed, "A good listener is not only popular everywhere, but after a while he gets to know something."

Trust me on this: It pays to listen—and it pays big.

## Watch How Others Do It

Successful salesmanship and marketing are totally dependent on good communications. It's not about manipulating or tricking people, it's about clearly and effectively relaying a message and receiving feedback.

If you study salesmanship and marketing—and you should, no matter what business you're in—you'll quickly realize that success in these fields is all about communications. As part of your mindfeed program, read books on these subjects. And then watch and learn from how the people you interact with use—or don't use—effective communication.

*Use your own buying experiences as lessons on effective selling.*

Use your own buying experiences as lessons. Whether you're buying a new car or a cup of coffee, evaluate what the salesperson said and did and how that made you respond. Then think about how you can use those techniques that you've found effective in your interactions with others.

Another great way to sharpen your communication skills is to study advertisements. What makes you react to a broadcast or print ad the way you do? Before you toss a direct-mail piece in the trash, study how it is put together.

Typically, a direct-mail advertisement will have a headline to get your attention, an opening that establishes rapport, body copy that gives you the information you need to know and answers your questions, a close that sums up the message or a pitch being conveyed, and a call to action that tells you what to do if you want to buy.

Use that same approach when you're negotiating to buy a piece of investment property. Get the seller's attention, create a bond by establishing rapport, explain that you want to buy the property and what the terms of your offer are, sum it up, and tell the seller what he or she needs to do to close the deal. It's a simple, organized process, and it works.

## Make It About the Other Person

It's human nature to go into a meeting or a negotiation focused on what you want rather than on what the other person wants. And maybe what you want really is the best thing all around. But if you ignore the concerns and feelings of others, if you just barge in making your points without listening, things aren't likely to end well.

Put yourself in the other person's place. You may find that you are dealing with sellers and even buyers who are in difficult circumstances; they have to trust you before you can close the deal. If you want people to feel comfortable with you, you have to go to where they are and build trust and rapport. Listen for their pacing, their speech patterns, their attitude. Pay attention to how they respond to you.

This process of noticing patterns is known as neurolinguistic programming (NLP)—something you should study as you practice mindfeed.

## Using NLP

Neurolinguistic programming was introduced in 1975 by Richard Bandler and John Grinder, who began modeling and duplicating the results of top communicators. One of the most important fundamentals of NLP is *modality*—the mode in which a person operates. Bandler and Grinder claim people have three major modes of taking in information: visually, auditorily, and kinesthetically.

Visual people process new information with images. When

standing or sitting, they tend to keep their bodies erect and their gazes alert. They are typically organized, well-groomed, and neat. They are bored by long verbal explanations and may have trouble remembering verbal instructions. They use words and phrases such as *see, look, watch, picture this*, and *it appears*.

Auditory people process with sound. They often talk to themselves and are easily distracted by noise. They learn by listening and can repeat things easily. They breathe from the middle of their chest. They use words and phrases such as *listen, speak, hear, said*, and *sounds like*.

Kinesthetic people process through touch and internal feelings. Their posture tends to be more slumped. They often move and speak slowly—a trait that can frustrate faster-paced visual and auditory folks. They tend to respond to touch, and they learn by doing. They use words and phrases such as *feelings, get in touch, get a handle on*, and *grasp*.

*Learn to recognize how people process information and adjust your approach accordingly.*

Most people operate in all three modes but tend to stay primarily in one. When you understand and can match a person's modality, it's easy to build rapport. By rapport, I'm referring to a relationship characterized by harmony, conformity, accord, or affinity. Essentially, it's when people like each other. Keep in mind that in general people who *are* like each other like each other; and when they *are not* like each other, their contrasting styles can cause friction.

Two key NLP techniques that I recommend you study and practice are *mirroring and matching* and *leading*.

When you *mirror*, you intentionally duplicate someone else's behavior. You can do this by copying the other person's gestures, posture, position, voice tone, and even breathing and speaking patterns. *Matching* involves responding to and duplicating how the other person processes information. For example, to match a visual person, you would say things like, "I see what you mean"; with an auditory person, you might say, "I hear what you're saying"; and with a kinesthetic person, you might say, "I feel like I understand what you're telling me."

*Leading* is used to attempt to change someone else's behavior. You begin by matching for a short period of time to establish rapport, before leading the other person by changing your behavior.

NLP is more than just a game of Simon Says. It's a way of reaching out to other people and proactively trying to establish a bond. Nor is mirroring alone enough; just crossing your legs or gesturing when the other person does isn't going to create an emotional connection. And if you're obvious about it, at best the other person will be amused; at worst, he'll be offended. But NLP can be useful to improve communication, by attempting to understand both the information and the communicator (the other person), and then structuring your own communication to that person.

There are other NLP techniques that you can use to improve communication and enhance your personal development. I've found it is a technology worth studying and using.

## e-NLP

NLP has traditionally been used as a tool for face-to-face communication. With the increasing popularity of e-mail, it makes sense to apply these same techniques to your electronic communications.

To use NLP in e-mail, don't look at *what* is being written, but rather at *how* it is being written. Spotting sensory words will tell you if the writer is visual, auditory, or kinesthetic. Use the same types of sensory language in your response.

Also look at the writer's sentence length and style, the degree of formality, his or her use of acronyms and abbreviations, and the general structure. Again, use a similar style when you reply.

If you receive an e-mail that's short and to the point, reply the same way. If the sender uses a formal salutation, begin your reply with something similar. If the e-mail is casual, make yours the same. When you apply NLP techniques to e-mail, you have another opportunity to build rapport.

## More Ways to Build Rapport

Rapport is defined as a relationship of mutual understanding or trust and agreement between people. It is absolutely essential that you be able to build rapport with buyers, sellers, and other investors. People want to do business with people they like, and people like people who show an interest in them.

It's not unusual for a new real estate investor to be so focused on the deal that he forgets the human side of the transaction. If people feel that all you care about is the money, they're probably going to choose to do business with someone else.

In addition to the behavioral techniques of NLP, show an interest in the other person as an individual. Ask questions—but avoid sounding like an inquisition.

"What do you do for a living?" is an acceptable question under almost any circumstances. Follow the answer with a comment and another question. "That sounds like an exciting job. Did you have to go to school for a long time?" Or "I have a friend who does that, and he loves it. Have you been doing this long?"

Look for visual conversation clues. If you're in a first-time meeting with a prospective seller in a public place, pay attention to how he's dressed. Does his shirt have a school or sports logo on it? Is he wearing a piece of jewelry, maybe a watch or ring, that would indicate an interest or hobby? If you're meeting with someone in her home or office, comment on a decorative element or furnishing, such as their photographs, wall hangings, plaques, trophies, or books. "That's a lovely picture; is it your family?" or "You must be a tennis player" are observations that will let you begin the rapport-building process.

Listen carefully to the answer; follow it up with another question or two. Be sure to answer any questions the other person may ask. Then gently move the conversation to the business at hand.

*When negotiating, ask questions as you go along to make sure you are understood.*

You will meet people who will tell you way more than you ever wanted to know about their personal life. Remember that when you are dealing with motivated sellers, their motivation may be causing serious emotional distress. If they need someone to listen, be that person. It's a small thing you can do to help someone who is having a rough time. It's happened to me, and my students have told me more stories than I can count about how they were able to make someone feel better just by showing an interest and listening, and then went on to close a win-win real estate deal.

This isn't something you can fake. If you don't genuinely care about people, they'll sense it. And if you do genuinely care about them, take a few moments to bond with them on a nonbusiness level before you get down to business.

## Be Sure Your Message Is Received

It's not enough to understand what others have said; you also need to make sure they understand you. The way to do that is by asking questions—and if you've established rapport, you'll be amazed at what you can ask and how much people will tell you.

Don't just ask the old standby questions like "Does that make sense?" and wait for them to bob their heads. When you're in a selling situation, you need to ask questions that will let you know if they really understand what you're saying and agree with you. Try questions like "Does this work with the situation you're in right now?" or "Is this something that fits your investment parameters?" or even "Can you do this deal?"

If the person likes and trusts you (rapport, remember), he'll answer you honestly. He'll say, "Yes, this works with my situation." Or "I'm really looking for an investment with a higher potential yield, even if it means greater risk." Or "I can't do this deal the way you've laid it out. I need more cash up front." In any of these cases, you have information you need so you can move to the next step.

## It Takes Practice

Most skills require practice to remain sharp. That's why performers rehearse, athletes exercise, and professionals take continuing education courses.

You can practice your communication skills by role-playing with your spouse or a close friend. Go through the entire scenario of whatever meeting you're planning to have, from greeting to rapport-building to your presentation and the close. Be sure you can comfortably and clearly explain all the aspects of the deal you're going to propose.

As your real estate investing business expands and you start applying new strategies, practice explaining them to someone you trust (or even a mirror) before you do it for real.

Keep on studying how others communicate. When you see an effective technique, learn to use it yourself. Talk—and listen—to your spouse, your kids, your friends, your colleagues. Consistently working on enhancing your communication skills will increase your earnings potential. It will also enrich your life, in more ways than you can imagine.

# CHAPTER 8

# You Need People

Don't try to go it alone. Sure, it's possible to become a millionaire by yourself—it's just not practical or effective. You'll be able to reach higher goals and do it faster if you take advantage of synergy. Remember, the whole is greater than the sum of the parts.

There are two aspects to this concept. The first is that you need to spend your time and energy doing things that will increase your wealth. Hire others to handle the menial, mundane, specialty, and non-revenue-generating tasks.

For example, keeping good records is essential. But don't spend your time sitting in front of the computer making entries into QuickBooks. Hire someone to do that for you, and spend those hours finding and negotiating real estate deals that will generate far more than what you are paying for the data entry.

Or let's say you find a property that needs some cosmetic fix-up before you can rent it or resell it. Hire somebody to do the painting

*Spend your time doing things that will increase your wealth; hire others to do non-revenue-generating work.*

and landscaping and cleanup while you're out finding another deal. Don't be penny-wise and pound-foolish. You might save a few hundred dollars by doing non-revenue-generating work yourself, but how much will you lose because you were typing or painting instead of actually building your wealth?

The second aspect is to build a Power Team. This is your team of professionals who are committed to helping you reach your goals. They're not doing this just to be nice; they're doing it because when you succeed, they succeed. Your real estate broker earns a commission when you buy and sell property; your mortgage broker earns a commission when you take out a loan; your banker makes money when you borrow; your insurance agent gets a commission on your policies; and so on. These people are all going to work hard for you, and they're not going to charge you a penny. I figured that out when I was young and just getting started—it fit right into my budget then, and it still does today.

## Building Your Power Team

Your Power Team doesn't have to be a formal team. This isn't a club with official membership. You don't need to ask someone if he'll be a part of your Power Team. Rather, you build relationships with people you can work with and who will support you. You may have companies or organizations, rather than individuals, as part of your Power Team. And your Power Team will be fluid and ever-evolving as your investing activities become increasingly sophisticated.

Many people build Power Teams instinctively. But when they understand the value of this resource, they get more deliberate about the process.

So who should be on your Power Team? Let's make a list:

*Appraisers.* Property appraisers know what's going on in the market because they are out there every day. They can share information on general trends and also be a source of specific referrals.

*Bankers.* You need at least one commercial banker on your Power Team to be a resource for you when you need bank loans (either mortgages or loans for other business purposes) and to be sure that you are getting the best possible services from your bank.

*Bird dogs.* These are the people who are out in the community and who can bring you deals. I talk more about bird dogs in Chapter 11—they can be utility workers, mail carriers, and other service workers who can tell you about potential deals they see in the neighborhoods where they are working. If you close a deal based on their lead, you pay them a referral fee.

*Build a Power Team of people who will benefit when you are successful.*

*Contractors.* If you're going to do rehabs or just hold rental properties, you need contractors to do the actual physical labor. A self-employed solo operator or a very small business will likely give you better prices and be more flexible to work with than a bigger operation. If you have rental properties, a good handyman is invaluable. If you're going to do rehabs, you'll need a team that includes a painter, plumber, electrician, drywall installer, and heat and air-conditioning technician.

*CPA who understands real estate.* The accountant who works with you on your record-keeping and taxes must know about real estate and the type of transactions you're doing.

*Hard money lender.* You need at least one hard money lender on your Power Team who can help you when you need this type of financing and refer you to other hard money sources as needed.

*Insurance agent.* Find a commercial agent who is knowledgeable about insuring investment real estate.

*Lawyers.* You need a real estate attorney to represent you as necessary in your transactions, and perhaps even to handle closings for you. As part of your network, you also need attorneys whose practices focus on other areas, such as divorce (marital law), bankruptcy, and probate, because they have clients who may need your help.

*Mortgage broker.* You can't afford to spend a lot of time chasing financing, so have a mortgage broker do it for you. The mortgage broker on your Power Team should understand what you do, enjoy working with investors, have access to nonconforming lenders, and also be willing to work with buyers who have poor credit. You may need more than one mortgage broker to accomplish your goals.

*Create a Power Team of positive people who understand your strategies and want to be a part of your success.*

*Other investors.* The other investors on your Power Team can include people who have money but aren't interested in the day-to-day work of finding and negotiating deals or managing property. You should also have at least one other investor who is using the same or similar strategies as you.

*Private money lenders.* These are the people who are willing to finance your deals but who don't operate as hard money lenders.

*Property managers.* Even if you prefer to manage your own holdings, build a relationship with property managers. They can help you with management issues, and they are likely to know when good investments are coming on the market.

*Real estate brokers and agents.* These are the folks who will help you find properties, make offers, and negotiate deals—and they get paid by the seller. There are many creative ways to work with real estate brokers and agents, and you may want more than one on your Power Team.

*Title company.* A title company conducts title searches, provides title insurance (usually paid for by the seller), and handles your closings. Be sure the title company on your Power Team will work with you according to your needs and strategies. For example, not all title companies will do double closings; be sure yours is comfortable with the process. Title companies can also be a source of leads when they see a deal falling through that you might be able to save.

Where do you find these people? You have to get out there and meet them. Join professional associations such as your local real estate investors club and property managers association. Call people who are running "I Buy" or "Money to Lend" ads. Talk to everyone you know and meet about what you do; you'll be surprised at who will step up and offer to help. You can also participate on the community bulletin board online at www.russwhitney.com—it's absolutely free, simple to use, and the quickest way possible to put my professional staff and thousands of my students on your Power Team today.

## Not Everyone Belongs

Who doesn't belong on your Power Team? That's simple: anyone who is negative and who thinks you can't achieve your goals.

# PART 2

# Real Estate
# Strategies

# CHAPTER 9

# Good Debt/Bad Debt

I t wasn't very long ago that debt was considered a shameful thing. In fact, the home mortgage as we know it didn't come into being until the 1930s. Prior to that, if you couldn't afford to pay cash for real estate, you rented.

Through the first half of the twentieth century, consumer borrowing was done on a very small scale. Some shopkeepers extended credit to individual customers on an informal basis, but the norm was for people to pay cash at the time they made their purchases. Smart business owners realized that extending credit inspired customer loyalty and increased sales, and it was that awareness that led to the introduction of credit cards in the 1920s. These initial cards were issued by companies to their customers for purchases made at those businesses. The first universal credit card was introduced by Diners Club in 1950, and bank credit cards came along about a decade later.

Mortgages made it possible for average wage earners to buy

their own homes, and that's good. They also made it possible for average people to invest in real estate—an opportunity that was previously unavailable to all but those who were already wealthy. Credit cards reduced the need to carry large amounts of cash and made it easier for people to track expenditures. However, they have also made it possible for average wage earners to get over their heads in debt.

When you have a mortgage on your house, clearly that's debt. When you owe $20,000 or more on multiple credit cards, that's also debt. But there is a dramatic difference between the two. Your house is an appreciating asset that is increasing in value as you pay off what you owe on it. More than likely, what you charged on those credit cards are depreciating assets that are worth far less than you paid for them by the time the bill comes in.

*Use debt to increase your wealth—not to buy depreciating assets.*

It's important to know how to look at debt properly. The point is not to be afraid of it, but to understand it and use it to your benefit. There really is such a thing as good debt. Good debt is money that you borrow to increase your personal wealth, such as loans you use to buy real estate.

## What's Bad About It?

Let's talk about bad debt. Every day, you are bombarded with "buy now, pay later" messages. They're on television, radio, billboards, newspapers—virtually everywhere you look. Not only are credit card companies urging you to charge what you want now and figure out how you're going to pay for it later, they're also competing for the debt you already have. How many times a week do you get a pitch for a new credit card with a special deal for balance transfers? By the way, you may be tempted to take advantage of those offers to try to reduce the amount of interest you pay, and, depending on your particular circumstances, that could be a smart strategy. But always read the fine print of the offer very carefully, because it's common for that super-low interest rate to be effective for a limited time, or you may have to pay a penalty if you don't carry a minimum balance (on which you are paying interest) for a specific period.

Any money that you owe for something that is not increasing in value is bad debt. Those consumer purchases—dinners out, clothes, household furnishings—that you put on a credit card and for which you pay interest on the unpaid balance are all bad debt. Bad debt is money you borrow to buy depreciating assets, which are things that go down in value as you continue to pay for them. Let me make it clear: I'm not suggesting that you shouldn't go out to dinner, buy clothes, or furnish your home—just don't borrow money to do it. I'm also not suggesting that you not use credit cards. In fact, there are many reasons why you should charge most of your purchases, such as easier record-keeping, rebates, various bonuses offered by the credit card companies, and consumer-protection services. Just be sure you never put a consumer purchase on a credit card that you can't pay off in full when the bill comes in.

## When Debt Is Good, It's Very Good

As I said, there really is such a thing as good debt. If you own a house, your mortgage is good debt because your home is more than likely appreciating in value as you are paying off the loan. If you own investment real estate that is appreciating in value and generating positive cash flow, the money you borrowed to make that purchase is good debt. But if you're still paying off the vacation you took last year with interest, that's bad debt—no matter how much fun you had.

It is the wise use of debt that helped most millionaires and billionaires build their fortunes. Consider these two scenarios:

Person A is sixty years old and has a good job at which he's worked all his adult life. He has lived in his house for thirty-two years, owns it free and clear, and drives an eight-year-old car that is also paid for. He usually pays cash, but when he charges, he pays the bill in full each month. He has no other debt and he's quite proud of that. His house is worth $200,000, his car is worth $4,000. He has $20,000 in a savings account and $300,000 in a 401(k), and his personal property is valued at $76,000. He's got a net worth of $600,000. At first, that sounds pretty good, but is it really? A third of his net worth is his house; if he needs cash and has to sell it, where will he live? What's going to happen to his income when he retires from that job—or what if he gets laid off? And just how far will $600,000 go these days, anyway?

*It doesn't matter who you borrow from, just make sure all of your loans are working for your benefit.*

Person B is also sixty years old with a house worth $200,000. He's been in the house ten years and owes $100,000 on it. Five years ago, he began investing in real estate, and now he also owns fifty residential real estate units (single-family homes and duplexes) valued at a total of $3 million. He owes a total of $2 million on those properties. His rental units generate $55,000 in positive cash flow a year. He also buys and sells other real estate, from which he nets another $150,000 a year. Without even considering his car, personal property, savings, or other investments, B has assets worth $3.2 million and liabilities of $2.1million, or a net worth of $1.1 million, plus income that is independent of a job.

A has no debt and $600,000 in assets. B has more than $2 million in debt and $3.2 million in income-producing assets. Who is in better financial shape?

Let's look into the future of both of these folks. Assuming their real estate increases in value just 5 percent per year, A will add $10,000 to his net worth next year (based on the current value of his house). Not a bad gain for doing nothing. But B's net worth will jump $160,000—also for doing nothing. I ask you again, who is in better financial shape, the person with no debt or the person who knows how to use debt wisely?

## Consider the Source—or Not

Is the quality of your debt affected by who you borrowed it from? Absolutely not. What's important is what you borrowed it for and if the terms are favorable. In Chapter 17, when we talk about financing your deals, we'll explore borrowing from nontraditional lenders and even using credit cards to make real estate purchases, and you'll learn the practical aspects of being a smart borrower.

When you make debt work for you, you're operating with the millionaire mindset.

▼

# CHAPTER 10

# Investor Eyes

Real estate millionaires train themselves how to look at property through the eyes of an investor, not the eyes of a consumer. Essentially, that means they have the ability to consider and evaluate real estate investments without getting emotional about them.

I can't count the number of times over the years that I have walked through potential investment properties with my students and watched the expressions on their faces. I can tell that many of them are visualizing what it would be like to live in that particular house—and if it's in a low- or moderate-income neighborhood, or in need of repair, the image isn't very appealing. Yet while they're turning their noses up, I'm trying to show them why the property is a great investment. Even when I say repeatedly, "You're not going to live here," it's hard for some people to think otherwise.

There's a big difference between how you look at investment property and how you look at property you're buying for yourself. The property you're buying to live in needs to suit your personal preferences and lifestyle. If you want to set up your business operation in a commercial location, the needs of your company will be a very important consideration. But when you're buying property as an investment, it's all about the numbers: What it will cost and how much revenue it will generate. If the numbers work, you buy. If they don't work, you don't buy. And it doesn't matter if the washing machine is in the garage or the utility room, or if the floor plan is formal or casual, or whether or not there's a place to display your collection of whatever it is that you collect.

*There's a big difference between how you look at investment property and how you look at property you're buying for yourself.*

## Know Your Market

This is old advice, but it bears repeating: Know your market. When you know your market, you can develop investor vision. And with investor vision, you can look at properties and clearly see their potential, or lack of potential.

Learning your market takes getting out of your own neighborhood and out of your comfort zone and into areas where you can create cash flow and build wealth. I'm not suggesting that you have to invest in neighborhoods that you're afraid to go into, but I'm sure there are plenty of neighborhoods in your area that are different from what you are familiar with. Get out there and get to know them.

Figure out who the other investors are and what they're doing. Are these people your competition? They can be—but if you're looking at the world through investor eyes, you'll see them as allies and resources.

Identify the trends in the area. How fast is property appreciating? How long are properties staying on the market before they sell? Is the area a target of a government revitalization plan? Is there a shift in property use—for example, is it a residential area that is gradually transitioning to commercial? What else is going on that could affect real estate uses and values?

There is absolutely no substitute for regularly driving through the areas where you are investing, looking at what's happening, talking to people, and truly knowing your market. You should also regularly meet with Realtors, mortgage brokers, bankers, appraisers, and other real estate professionals who have their fingers on the pulse of the market. For more about building relationships that will help you in this area, see Chapter 8.

## Higher and Better Use

In my book *Building Wealth*, I discussed the concept of higher and better use at a very basic level. I explained how you could convert a single-family home into a rooming house and substantially increase your positive cash flow. For example, if you have a three-bedroom house in a working-class neighborhood, you might be able to rent it for $800 a month. But let's say you convert the living room to another bedroom and rent those four bedrooms with kitchen privileges for $100 a week each. You've just doubled your revenue. Of course, you have to be sure zoning regulations will allow such a conversion, and you need to consider your costs. But the basic principle of higher and better use is to buy property for its present value—or less—and then figure out how to use the property in a different way to create more value without spending a lot of money.

Here's another example: Let's say you find an older, two-family home that has a huge attic. You could spend $20,000 to convert the attic into a third unit, increase your cash flow, and add $100,000 in value to the property. Essentially, look at every investment you make and ask yourself if you are getting the absolute highest and best use possible from the property.

Recently, two of my students did their first deal, a one-up, one-down duplex in Massachusetts. It was on the market for $419,000; they negotiated to $385,000 with 5 percent down. They spent about three months and $20,000 on repairs, then sold the units as condos for a total of $525,000—that's a $120,000 profit.

On a larger scale, you may find an apartment building for sale and convert it to condominiums or a co-op. Let's say you buy a fifty-unit apartment complex for $3 million. If you do a condo conversion and sell the units for $100,000 each, your gross profit will be $2 million. Depending on the neighborhood, even an old motel has the potential to be converted into apartments or condos for a higher and better use—and substantial profits.

*Figure out who the other investors in your market are and what they're doing.*

One of the biggest real estate trends right now is apartment-to-condo conversions. They have a tremendous amount of profit potential, but you need to do your homework before you buy. Put together a thorough plan on exactly what you intend to do, including how you will market the property afterward. Be sure the necessary zoning is in place and that you can obtain whatever permits will be needed.

On bigger land deals (which we'll discuss at length in later chapters), an urban planner can be invaluable in helping you determine the highest and best possible use of the property. He'll have the resources to study not only that particular piece of property but the surrounding market, and he'll be able to tell you what will work and what won't work on the site.

The trend of inner-city gentrification is another classic example of higher and better use. Old industrial cities are tearing down abandoned warehouses and replacing them with high-end condos and shops. Recently, I was in Hoboken, New Jersey. I hadn't been there in years, and I remembered it as a not-so-pretty industrial city with lots of waterfront warehouses. Today, those warehouses are gone, and it's absolutely beautiful—lovely homes and condos, parks, stores, and everything is clean and well maintained. The civic leaders and developers behind that incredible transformation clearly understand the principle of higher and better use.

*Never buy a property without a primary and backup plan for getting out of it.*

When you are dealing with developed property, you have a lot more restrictions when it comes to higher and better use. But when you are looking at raw land, the possibilities are limited only by your imagination. Every land deal I have been involved in has been profitable because I've looked for a higher and better use for the property.

I'm involved in the development of an upscale residential community called Tranquility Bay Florida. Someone brought me a deal on a beautiful tract of land on the Gulf of Mexico that had a straight canal cut into it to allow boat access to the Gulf. It's a total of 74 acres with 20 acres left natural. In that natural area are walking paths and a 4.5-acre lake, making a very attractive common amenity.

To develop that property as it was would have been a profitable deal. But more waterfront lots would be better, so we applied for and received permission to extend the canal and make it a horseshoe shape. The community has a total of 57 lots; 5 are bayfront and 46 are on the canal with bay access. By having the vision to extend the canal, we have enhanced the value of the entire development. When we bought the land, the individual lots were worth maybe $50,000. Now the off-water lots are worth more than $250,000, the canal lots are worth about $500,000, and the bayfront lots are worth $1 million. It's the same land, just higher and better use.

*Aerial view of the Tranquility Bay site in early stages of development.*

## With Investor Eyes
## Come Investor Strategies

As you learn to see the way investors do, you also need to learn to operate the way successful investors do. Here are some basic investor strategies that are habits to people with the millionaire mindset:

*Always have an exit strategy.* Never get into a property unless you know how you're going to get out of it—and what your backup plan is if that doesn't work. You should have an exit strategy even when you buy property to hold—your strategy may be to put tenants in the property for ten years, let it appreciate while the rents pay down the mortgage, then sell and take your profits. If you're

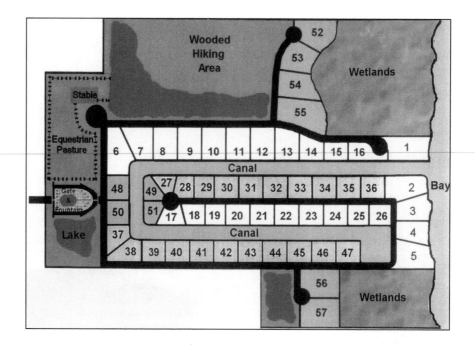

*Tranquility Bay site plan showing extended canal.*

buying for a quick-turn, how will you sell? Will you syndicate it? Bring investors in to take you out of it? Lease-option it to another investor or an end user? As we talk about investment strategies in later chapters, we'll also talk about some exit strategies.

*Don't get emotionally involved with your investment properties.* How can you get emotionally involved with land and brick and mortar? It happens all the time, and when it does, the investor is almost certain to take a financial hit. The most common example of this is buying residential property and spending too much on fixing it up. You're not going to live in the house, so don't put up wallpaper when paint will do, don't spend money on upgraded fixtures when midrange products will suffice, and don't let the property reflect your personality—it needs to be neutral so it will appeal to a wide range of potential tenants and/or investors.

*Keep your relationship with your tenants on a business level.* Your tenants are not your friends, they're your tenants. You can certainly be friendly, and you definitely want to be pleasant and cordial, but don't step over the line to friendship. If you do that, it becomes very difficult to enforce the business side of your relationship. So if you have a tenant you've become friends with, and he suddenly starts disturbing the neighbors with loud music at night or junk cars parked on the lawn, or she can't pay the rent when it's due and wants permission to pay a couple of weeks late without any sort of penalty, it's going to be hard for you to insist that they follow the rules and the terms of their lease. But if you've kept your relationship on a business level, it's much easier to tell tenants to turn down the noise, get rid of the junk, and pay their rent on time or face the consequences (such as late fees and even eviction).

*Always be ready to take advantage of opportunities when they arise—even unexpected ones.*

*Always keep your properties well maintained.* Whether you invest in low-, moderate-, or upper-income neighborhoods, maintain your properties. They should always be clean and in good repair. If they're not, some tenants may use that as an excuse for not paying their rent. Also, by taking care of your properties, you'll attract a higher caliber of tenant. It's not much different from owning a convenience store. If you keep the store clean and crisp, your customers will feel good about shopping there. If it's dirty and dingy, you'll probably lose business. Good landlords usually have a waiting list of good tenants for their properties.

*Be ready to grow.* Most investors start small and plan to grow. That's an excellent strategy, but don't fall into the trap of letting yourself get stuck at a level that won't meet your goals. Don't let yourself get complacent and don't shortchange your goals because you're comfortable and making "enough." It's quite possible that your growth opportunities will come to you when you're least expecting them, so be ready for them.

*Create a plan and stay focused.* Investors with the millionaire mindset take the time to formulate a solid plan and then implement it. Put your plan on paper and refer to it regularly. Recognize that people usually get off track just an inch or two at a time and don't realize it until they are miles away from where they should be. If you routinely compare your performance to your goals and work your plan, you'll stay on track.

*Operate with integrity.* Be honest and fair with everyone you do business with. Never do a deal unless everyone involved is a winner. Do the right thing just because it's the right thing, and it will come back to you in more ways than you can imagine.

# CHAPTER 11

# Buying Right:
# You *Can* Get It Wholesale

Though they may not always *get* their money until the property is sold, successful real estate investors always strategize to *make* their money when they buy. And in many situations, they don't even need to actually formalize the purchase to walk away with a substantial profit on a real estate deal.

In Chapter 2, we talked briefly about wholesale buying, and I think the subject deserves a significant amount of explanation. This is one of the most powerful strategies in real estate investing, and it really is something you can do with no money and poor credit.

For years, wholesale-buying "experts" have taught the same old stale strategy: Look for run-down, boarded-up, abandoned properties, try to find the owners, and then buy them for a fraction of fair market price. The biggest problem with the approach is that too many of those properties are in low- and moderate-income areas— neighborhoods where new investors might not feel comfortable spending a lot of time. Sure, you might be able to pick up an abandoned property that's been used by vagrants and crack addicts in a bad neighborhood for pennies on the dollar. You could fix it up and rent it out, or quick-turn it to another investor or even a homeowner, and you could make a profit more than worth your time. Certainly, a lot of investors are successfully doing this, and I explained the strategy in detail in my best-selling book *Millionaire Real Estate Mentor*.

*Wholesale investing strategies work in all types of neighborhoods with properties in all price ranges.*

Does this mean that you can't use wholesaling strategies in working-class, middle-class, or even upper-level income areas? No. An emphatic, absolute *no*. Wholesaling works in nice neighborhoods every bit as well—and often even more profitably—as it works in not-so-nice neighborhoods. And while I recommend that you begin by focusing on vacant properties until you get some experience, you can also do great wholesale deals on occupied properties.

## Why Wholesale?

When you do wholesale investing the way I'm going to show you, you have some very clear advantages. The most important is that you can do it without cash (except for the nominal deposit you may have to put up when you sign the contract—and that's usually just $100 or so). You'll make your profits quickly, usually within a few weeks. You do, however, need to know how to buy at a discount and turn the deal fast.

Basically, wholesale properties have a seriously motivated seller who often needs to get rid of the house yesterday. The property may be in poor condition, which means the average home buyer doesn't want it. Most real estate agents insist that the owner fix up the property before they'll accept the listing; when the owner doesn't have either the cash or the interest in doing the fix-up, the property is a great opportunity for a wholesale real estate investor.

Many investors routinely buy wholesale for their own portfolios. What they typically do is buy a property at a discount with short-term financing, because traditional financing is often difficult to get for these properties. Then they do whatever repair and rehab is necessary to get the property to a level so it will qualify for traditional financing. They take out a new mortgage for 80 or 90 percent of the market value (which they have forced up substantially by fixing up the property), pay off the initial loan and repair costs, and they're left with the rest of the loan money to use however they choose. They put a tenant in the property, let the rent pay down the mortgage while the property appreciates, and enjoy the cash flow until whatever point in the future they decide to sell.

Could you do this? Sure, but it usually takes access to at least some cash. Can you make money with wholesale strategies if you don't have any (or much) cash? Definitely. Here's how:

## Don't Buy

When you find a great wholesale deal, don't buy it. Instead, get it under contract and assign that contract to another investor for a fee.

Here's what that strategy would look like (and I'm going to explain how to do each of these steps):

1. You find a vacant house that needs a little bit of repair.
2. You locate the owner and determine that he is willing to sell.
3. Based on your knowledge of the area, you make an offer contingent on an inspection of the property.

4. If the seller is willing to accept your offer, you arrange to meet him at a neutral place to sign the contract.

5. You could go look at the property now, but it's not necessary.

6. You contact other investors (and I'm going to explain how to do that later in this chapter) with the basic information about the deal and offer to assign the contract for a fee.

7. When an investor indicates interest, you arrange to either show her the property or tell her to go look at it on her own.

8. If she wants to do the deal, you assign your purchase contract to her and collect your fee.

Here's what the numbers could look like for a house in a middle-income neighborhood: Let's say the average sale price for homes in the area is $110,000 to $130,000. You find a house that has been vacant for five months because the previous owner died and the heir hasn't had time to do anything with it. The house needs about $9,000 in fix-up and deferred maintenance, and its after-repair value (ARV) would be $120,000. You offer $84,000 (or 70 percent of the ARV) and promise to close within thirty days. The owner accepts your offer, and you sign a purchase contract. You have an investor who is interested in the property, and you offer to assign the contract to her for a $5,000 fee. She agrees, you do the necessary paperwork and collect your fee, and she closes on the deal and takes ownership of the property.

*Generate immediate cash by finding deals and assigning the contracts to other investors for cash.*

The seller of the house is happy because he's rid of a problem, he didn't have to do any work on the property, and he didn't have to deal with getting it listed and all the other hassles that come with showing a property to prospective buyers. The investor is happy because she didn't have to spend any time looking for a great investment, and now she has a property that cost her $89,000 to buy, plus $9,000 to repair (a total of $98,000), and will be worth $120,000 as soon as the work is done—which means in a very short time, the investor will have $22,000 in equity in the property. And you have $5,000 in cash that you made in just a couple of weeks.

Everybody is a winner. And deals like this are happening every day all over the country. Recently, one of my students in Iowa found a three-bedroom home with a fair market value of $39,000. The seller was behind in payments, and the house needed some "TLC." My student got the property under contract for $21,000 and the very next day assigned that contract for $2,200—not a bad rate of pay for a day's work, is it?

Let's go through the process step by step.

## Build an Investor Database

You need to build a database of investors who may be interested in buying contracts from you. There are plenty of investors out there who would jump on a good deal, especially if they didn't have to take the time to find it and negotiate it. Set up a database in your computer or PDA (personal digital assistant). The information you collect on each investor should include:

Full name
Address
Business phone
Home phone
Cell phone or pager
Fax
E-mail

Investing areas of interest

Preferred location

Preferred property type

Preferred financing (access to cash and lenders)

You should also include a place to make notes on any transactions you do with this particular individual.

When you find a good deal, you can either send out a fax or e-mail blast to everyone in your database, or you can contact investors individually. Do these investors want to hear from you?

*View other investors as resources, not as competitors.*

You bet they do. Think about it from this perspective: Wherever you happen to be in the development of your own real estate investing business, if someone brought you a great deal and you had the financial wherewithal to buy the property, would you do it? Of course you would.

You may not have the financial resources to make such investments right now. I understand—that's why I'm explaining how you can assign contracts for cash, so you can get the money you need to make longer-term wealth-building investments.

Before we talk about how to find other investors, let's talk about how to view them. They are colleagues and opportunities, not competition. Will you occasionally compete with them for the same deal? Probably. But then, a month later, you might be buying a property from them or selling one to them. Other investors are not your enemies—they are resources that you can use for win-win results.

So where do you find these other investors? They are all around you. Here are some ways to identify them and get their information:

*"I Buy" signs and car magnets.* Look for the signs and car magnets that investors display that say "I buy houses cash, any condi-

tion, call John" and give the investor a call. Tell him you saw his sign and you'd like to get more information about what he does. Take good notes, and let him know that when you have something that meets his parameters, you'll be back in touch.

*The "For Rent" and "For Sale" sections of your local newspaper.* Read the "For Rent" section for property owners and look in the "For Sale" section for "Rent to Own" offers. In the next chapter, you'll learn how to do "rent to own" deals and why they're so lucrative. In the meantime, these are two areas where you'll find real estate investors who are active in the area and who may be interested in properties to buy and hold.

*Local real estate investor clubs.* Most metropolitan areas have one or more real estate investor clubs, along with other organizations that serve investors, such as the apartment owners association and the property managers association. Joining these groups is a great way to meet other investors, as well as other people who are candidates for your Power Team (a concept we discussed in more detail in Chapter 8).

*Foreclosure sales (courthouse auctions).* Most of the people who attend foreclosure sales are serious investors. A good way to get to know them is to watch the auction process and see what they're bidding on. That will tell you what they like to invest in, and if it matches your own preferences, you should introduce yourself. Wait until the auction is over (never distract an investor in the middle of the bidding process) and give the investor your business card. If he picked up a good deal on a property, congratulate him. If he lost to another investor, commiserate with him. Then casually ask him a few questions about his business; chances are, he'll offer you his card. Don't take a lot of time at this point. Instead, let him know you'd like to talk more later, and then follow up.

# Finding Deals

As you're building your investor database, you should be out there looking for deals—for two reasons: First, you've got to have a deal to make any money; and second, while you're looking for deals, you'll find more investors in the process.

The traditional ways to find wholesale deals include:

- ▼ Real estate agents and brokers who can help you find properties listed at below market value. You can find those who like to work with investors at your local real estate investors club.
- ▼ Ads in daily newspapers, weekly shoppers, and real estate publications. Look for ads with language that indicates the seller is motivated. Just keep in mind that if you've seen it, so have a lot of other investors.
- ▼ "For Sale" signs in front of properties. These could be either Realtor signs or "For Sale by Owner" signs. As with newspaper ads, lots of other people have also seen these signs, and many of these owners are not strongly motivated.
- ▼ Foreclosures. Check the legal notices for foreclosure announcements. These deals are great if you have cash.
- ▼ Title companies. The clerks at title companies can be a great resource for tips on deals that have fallen through and need an investor who can step in and move quickly.
- ▼ Code-enforcement officials. Properties that have been cited for code violations are often strong candidates for a wholesale deal. If you get to know the folks at your local code-enforcement agency, they may let you know when a property in your target area has been tagged before it becomes common knowledge.

▼ Appraisers. Property appraisers know what's happening in the market—after all, that's their job. They can let you know about prospective deals.

▼ Property managers. Property managers are often the first to know when their clients—the property owners—are ready to sell.

These are all great methods that work well, but there are even better ways to find wholesale deals. First, let's discuss the types of areas where you're likely to find wholesale opportunities.

## Know the Neighborhood

There are four basic types of single-family residential neighborhoods: low-income, working-class, middle-income, and upper-income. Each will have similar characteristics regardless of the city or town; the primary difference when it comes to geography is the price range. For example, low-income houses in California typically cost substantially more than low-income houses in Des Moines. But other than the prices, everything else is essentially the same.

Low-income neighborhoods have some of the best opportunities for wholesale deals. Typically, these are the neighborhoods that have been around for what seems like forever, and the streets are often named after trees and dead presidents. Because the neighborhoods are older, so are the buildings. Many houses in low-income neighborhoods may be vacant and boarded up, and often the crime rate will be higher than in other areas.

Of the houses in low-income neighborhoods, what we typically find (although this can vary by region) is that about 55 percent are rentals, 25 percent are owner-occupied, and 20 percent are vacant.

The investors who own those rentals are excellent prospects for properties you may find and get under contract.

Working-class neighborhoods are also great for wholesaling, as well as for retailing (selling to the end user/homeowner) and holding for rentals. These are typically older neighborhoods that used to be considered middle-income. You can drive through these areas and know the occupations of the residents by the vehicles parked in the driveways: usually police cars and working vans and trucks.

Of these properties, it's common for nearly half to be rentals, half to be owner-occupied, and a few (usually about 5 percent) to be vacant. There is generally less inventory and plenty of competition, because other investors love these neighborhoods, too. But don't let that stop you from trying to invest in these areas; if you follow my advice, you can do it successfully.

Middle-income neighborhoods are the most popular property type when measuring growth patterns. They're usually newer, which means the owners have little or no equity. You may not be able to do much wholesale buying in middle-income neighborhoods, but you can still make money in these areas—I'll explain how to do that in the next chapter. Typically, in middle-income neighborhoods, 10 percent or fewer are rentals, 90 percent are owner-occupied, and maybe 1 or 2 percent are vacant. When you see a new Starbucks, Lowe's, Home Depot, or Wal-Mart, chances are you'll find middle-income neighborhoods very close by.

Upper-income neighborhoods have larger, more expensive, more feature-rich homes than middle-income. You'll rarely find a wholesale deal in an upper-income neighborhood, but they do happen. Not long ago, one of my company's mentors (the trainers who go out and work one-on-one with our students) found a house listed in Naples, Florida, for $1.4 million. He got the property under contract for $640,000 with 20 percent owner financing and wholesaled the deal to another investor for a $25,000 profit. You can also do deals in upper-income neighborhoods using the techniques in the next chapter. First, let's talk about how you can put together a wholesale deal.

## What Do You Say to the Seller?

In most cases, your initial conversation with a seller will be on the phone, and most of the time, the seller will call you. It happens that way when you properly market your business, and I'm going to tell you how to do that.

In most cases, your conversation will begin with the seller asking how your program works. You should respond with a clear overview, which is that you buy houses with either cash or terms. When you buy with cash, you need to buy at a discount. Then get some information on the property. If this is a property you've found yourself and the owner is responding to your efforts to contact him, you already have some answers. But before you can make an offer, you need to know:

▼ Property address
▼ Name and contact information (home phone, work phone, and cell phone) for the owner or owners (you need to know the names of everyone who has an ownership interest in the house, because they all have to agree to the sale)
▼ Is the property occupied or vacant?
▼ Is it a single-family home, duplex, or multi-unit building?
▼ Type of construction (brick or frame)
▼ Total square feet
▼ Number of bedrooms and baths
▼ If it has a garage or carport (or if such a space has been converted)
▼ If it has central heat and air

- ▼ What year it was built
- ▼ What the tax appraisal is
- ▼ What the market value is
- ▼ If there is a mortgage on the property, and if so, the amount and payments
- ▼ If there are any other liens on the property that would have to be settled before a sale could close

You should also ask if the property needs any repairs, and if so, how much the owner estimates they will cost. Sellers almost always underestimate the cost of repairs, but having that number still helps you calculate your offer.

With this information, you can quickly calculate your offer. Explain that you make your living helping people solve their real estate problems, and that when you make a purchase on a cash basis, you must do so at a discount. Then make your offer—right then, while you're on the phone.

Once the seller accepts your offer, make arrangements to meet with him to get the contract signed. For your personal safety and security, I recommend that you choose a mutually convenient public place, such as a restaurant or coffeehouse. If you decide to go to the seller's residence, don't go alone—whether you are male or female, always bring someone with you.

Once the contract is signed, you can invest time in personally looking at the property—but it's not essential even at that point. My students routinely put together wholesale deals, assign the contracts, and make $4,000 to $6,000 per transaction without ever seeing the property involved.

When you make your offer, how much of a discount should you try to get? That depends on the market plus the property's condition and immediate area. The overall national average discount on a wholesale real estate transaction is 30 percent below retail value plus repairs. So if the retail value of the property is $100,000 and the seller estimates it needs $8,000 in repairs, you would offer $62,000.

Of course, the stronger the market, the lower the discount. And in weak markets, you can get a better discount. However, keep in mind that the higher the discount you ask for up front, the fewer deals you'll end up closing. The key to success in real estate is to put together deals where everyone wins, and when you discount the property too deeply, even a motivated seller may turn down your offer.

Once you have the property under contract, the seller will start spending the money in his mind. So if you do have to go back and renegotiate the contract, you usually won't have any trouble.

## Conditions of Your Contract

The contract you use is an "Offer to Purchase Real Estate," and it needs to be only one page long. The essential elements the contract should include are:

- ▼ Your name followed by the phrase "and/or assigns." This is what allows you to assign the contract to another investor for a fee.
- ▼ The seller/owner's name (or names, if the property is owned by more than one person).
- ▼ The address of the property, including number, street, city or town, county, and state.
- ▼ Allow space for the full legal description and note that it will be provided by the closing agent.

- ▼ The total purchase price offered, the deposit paid with the contract, and the balance due at closing.
- ▼ The specific terms of the transaction, such as if the offer is subject to financing or a home inspection report, and that both buyer and seller will pay normal closing costs.
- ▼ When the closing will occur (generally, on or about thirty days from contract acceptance) and where (the name and address of your title agent).
- ▼ A clause stating that the offer is subject to your inspection and approval of written bids for necessary repairs within fourteen business days.
- ▼ A clause stating that the seller will provide access (a key) to the property on acceptance of the contract.
- ▼ A list of any items that will be conveyed with the property, such as appliances, fixtures, and furnishings.
- ▼ A place for your signature and date, and the owner/seller's signature(s) and date.

Have the seller sign first, then you sign and give him a copy. A sample offer to purchase real estate form can be found in Appendix C.

## The Importance of the Inspection Clause

The inspection clause—not the "home inspection report" but your personal inspection of the property and approval of written bids for necessary repairs—is what protects you. During that period, if you realize your numbers don't work for any reason, you can attempt to renegotiate, and if that doesn't work, you can walk away. This also gives you time to run a preliminary title search to confirm what liens and other encumbrances may exist. If you find something the owner failed to disclose—whether it was deliberate, because he forgot, or because he didn't know about a particular lien—you can decide if you want to renegotiate the terms or cancel the contract.

The student from Iowa I mentioned earlier ran into a situation like this and managed to make it profitable. The property's fair market value was $62,000, but the owner was falling behind in his payments and the house needed some work. My student got it under contract for $39,365 and during the inspection period found an undisclosed lien for $26,000. He extended his contract with the owner to give himself time to deal with the situation, negotiated a payoff of $7,000 on the lien, then assigned the contract and earned a net profit of $5,167.

Note that your inspection period is "fourteen business days"— not calendar days. That gives you almost three weeks to find another investor to assign your contract to. If you can't find another investor, you have the option to close on the deal yourself (if you have the cash or can get the financing) or to cancel the contract.

This clause is why you can sign a contract without seeing the property first. There is no reason for you to spend a lot of time looking at properties, getting repair estimates, or looking for other investors to buy the contract if you don't know that your offer will be accepted. You want to have the property under your control with a contract before you show it to another investor. Never put yourself in the position of telling another investor you have a great deal—and then having to go back and say you're sorry but the seller wouldn't accept your offer so the deal fell through.

On the other hand, in fairness to the owner/seller, you don't want to keep the property off the market for an excessive period of time—and you should explain that when you are signing the contract. Say something like, "My associates and I need some time to inspect the property and get repair estimates to be sure we can make this deal work. We're going to do this as quickly as we can. We want to be fair, and that's why you'll know, and we'll know, if we can make it work within fourteen business days."

## Why Do Sellers Accept Discounted Prices?

Why would anyone sell a property for less than it's worth? Because they are motivated. They may be motivated because the property needs repairs that they don't have the time, money, or inclination to do themselves. They may be motivated because they need cash quickly. They may be motivated because they just don't want to be bothered with the property.

*To find out how motivated a seller is, simply ask why they're selling.*

You should be able to tell very quickly how motivated a seller is. If the seller is not motivated, move on to the next deal. Without a motivated seller, you can't put together a wholesale deal, so don't waste your time or theirs.

To determine their motivation, find out if they simply *want* to sell or if they *have* to sell. All you have to do is ask. Most people will tell you far more than you want to know about their situation. If you listen sympathetically and then work to help them solve the real estate part of their problem, you'll make money and everybody will win.

The key is motivation, and I can't stress that enough. Consider this scenario: Sam is getting ready to retire in about six months. He and his wife are empty nesters, and they think they'd like to move into a place that's smaller and requires less maintenance than their current house. Sam has taken excellent care of the property, it's in a great neighborhood, and the market is strong. Is Sam motivated to sell? No, not a bit.

But let's say Sam has been retired for three years, has a pension that isn't quite meeting his expenses, isn't physically able to take care of his property and knows it's deteriorating, has tried to list the house with a Realtor but the agent wants him to do thousands of dollars in fix-up and repairs first, and he needs cash so he can move out of state to live with one of his grown children. Is he motivated? You bet.

When you have a motivated seller, you need to clearly explain what you do and how it can benefit the seller. You don't need to make a speech; just simple conversation will do. Explain that as real estate investors, you and your associates make your living buying properties below market value, fixing them up, and either reselling them or renting them out. When they sell their property to you, the deal will close quickly, usually within thirty days; they don't have to pay a Realtor commission (assuming, of course, that the property is not listed with a Realtor); they don't have to go through the hassle of showing the house to prospective buyers; and they don't have to spend any time or money on fix-up.

## More Ways to Find Deals

Now that you understand how wholesaling works as a great cash flow generator, let's talk about more ways to find deals.

### Marketing

If nobody knows that you're a real estate investor, how will anyone know to call you when they have a property to sell? Marketing is the most critical part of building a successful real estate investing business. It costs money to do, but it's money well spent.

Earlier in this chapter, I mentioned finding other investors through their "I Buy" signs. You need to have your own signs out in the neighborhoods you're targeting. Put your signs everywhere you possibly can—along busy streets, on trees and utility poles, even on vacant houses. Get magnetic signs and attach them to your car. Sure, they might look a little silly, but you won't mind that after the first deal you do because someone saw your car in the parking lot at the grocery store, wrote down the number, and called you. Pass out flyers. Get business cards printed and give at least two to everyone you meet—including store clerks and restaurant wait staff. Run "I Buy" ads in local publications, including the daily paper's real estate section, the weekly shoppers, and any specialty publications that property sellers might read.

When someone calls you, always ask how they heard about you so you can track the effectiveness of your marketing efforts. Another way to do this is to put different names in ads and on signs. If a caller asks for Sam, for example, you'll know he's seen your ad in the weekly shopper; if he asks for Cheryl, you'll know he's calling from a sign. And your response is "I'm sorry, Cheryl isn't in at the moment. My name is George, and I work with her. May I help you?"

*Marketing is the most critical part of building a successful real estate investing business.*

Make sure that the number you put on your signs and in your ads is a number you answer. The advice "answer your phone" seems incredibly basic, but plenty of investors routinely let these calls go to voice mail and miss out on some great deals. Put yourself in the position of someone who is responding to an "I buy real estate, fast closing" ad. He's calling because he needs to sell his property quickly. Do you think he wants to leave his name and number and wait for you to call him back? No. He wants to talk to

---

### Sample "I Buy" Ads for Signs, Flyers, and Postcards

I buy houses cash or terms!
Fast Closing!
Call Fred (444) 123-4567

Julie buys houses!
Fair offers, fast closing
Any area or condition
Call (999) 777-6543

I buy houses, condos,
and multi-unit properties!
Cash or terms, quick closing
Call Susan (333) 678-1234

$$$ CASH $$$
For your house!
Any condition or area.
Call Max (222) 789-5432

Cash for houses!
Any area, any condition
Call John (555) 987-6543

---

somebody right now, and if you're not available, he'll probably just hang up and go on to the next ad.

You need to be willing to invest time and money in your marketing plan. You cannot sit back and figure that you'll get some signs made up after you do a deal or two and get some cash—it's going to be very difficult to do those first few deals if nobody knows who you are and what you do. Those with a millionaire mindset understand the value of marketing.

## Networking

Some of your best deals will come through networking, because beginning your relationship with the seller based on a referral automatically generates a higher level of trust. Everyone you know should understand that you're the go-to person if anyone has a piece of problem real estate, and that you will compensate them if you close on a deal they refer to you.

You can also set up your own bird-dog program. Look for people who work or spend time in your target areas and let them know you'll pay a reward if they bring you a deal you can close. Your bird dogs will include: mail carriers, meter readers, lawn-service workers, trash collectors, newspaper carriers, pizza delivery drivers, and phone and cable company workers.

Build relationships with attorneys who may be able to recommend your services to their clients. Send letters of introduction to attorneys who specialize in real estate, estate planning, probate, bankruptcies, foreclosure, and divorce. Attorneys can't accept a referral fee, but let them know you will retain them to review any contracts related to a transaction they refer to you.

Another professional group worth networking with is bail bond agents. These are the folks who post bond for people who have been arrested on criminal charges, and they often have property they have received from their clients that they'd like to sell.

Finally, you want to get to know private lenders and hard money lenders who may have had to foreclose on a loan. In most cases, these people are not interested in owning property and just want to recover the amount owed—and you can help them.

## Tracking Vacant Houses

Your better deals will often come from properties that were not on the market when you found them. When you're looking for whole-sale real estate deals, I recommend that you start out focusing on vacant single-family houses. The deals are quicker and cleaner, the sellers are generally more motivated, and you don't have to manage the variable of waiting for an occupant to move out. Also, the majority of the people in the United States live in single-family homes. Overall, this type of property has the highest demand, has the most available programs for financing, appreciates the fastest, is fairly easy to rent to stable tenants, and is easier to get out of if you need to. For non-wholesale deals, I recommend starting with properties ranging from single-family up to four-unit buildings.

One way to find vacant houses is to regularly drive through the neighborhoods where you want to invest and look for indications that a house is vacant. A more refined approach is to ask a real estate agent for a list of properties in your target areas that have been on the market longer than the average sale time. Go look at those houses—they might turn out to be something you're interested in. But also look at nearby properties; chances are, if there's one property in a neighborhood that isn't selling, there will be others, and those others may or may not be listed with a Realtor. We teach this technique in our training, and when we take students out on property tours, we almost always find an unlisted vacant house within a block or two of the listed house.

What should you look for to determine if a house is vacant? An overgrown, neglected yard; newspapers and flyers piled in the driveway; mail not picked up; telephone directories on the porch; no curtains on the windows, or the windows are broken; code-enforcement tags on the door; boarded-up windows and doors; and abandoned vehicles and other junk in the yard.

When you find a vacant house, you need to track down the owner to see if he is interested in selling. In most areas, property records are available online, so a simple computer check will tell you who owns the property and where the tax bills are being sent. Or you can mail a postcard to the property address with the words "address service requested" on the front. The post office will advise you of the forwarding address if one is on file.

You can also check with the neighbors on both sides of and across the street from the property. You might be surprised at how generous they'll be with information—they'll probably tell you how long the property has been vacant and whatever else they happen to know about the owner and the situation.

When you find the owner, send her a postcard or letter explaining that you noticed the property, you're in the business of solving real estate problems, and if she's interested in selling, she should please contact you—and list your contact information, including a phone number, mailing address (never your home address), and Web site if you have one. If she's not interested in selling, she'll probably ignore your letter. So if she calls, you'll know immediately that you have a seller who is at least somewhat motivated. Start asking questions and listening carefully to the answers, and you'll quickly determine if there is a deal to be made.

## It's Contract Time

Once the owner/seller has accepted your offer on the phone, set up a time to meet with him as soon as possible to "do the paperwork." This phrase is less intimidating than saying you need him to sign the contract.

*Never "sign contracts," just "do the paperwork."*

When it comes to the contract document, the simpler, the better. You can get blank contracts from office supply stores, your local Board of Realtors office, and closing agents. Or you can download the contract from www.russwhitney.com. Many successful investors take the key information from boilerplate contracts and create their own documents.

Remember that many generic contracts contain a number of clauses that may not apply to your transactions, but you should be absolutely certain before you delete a clause that you really don't need it.

The two most important things you must have in every single one of your contracts are:

First, the buyer should be shown as your name followed by "and/or assigns." This is what allows you to assign the contract to another investor.

Second, you must have your escape or "subject to" clause. This is the clause that lets you walk away from the deal if you have to.

When you sit down with the seller, take the time to go through each item in the contract and make sure he understands what it means. If you make any changes or deletions to the form, you should both initial them. You should put your deposit with the closing agent (typically either the title company or real estate attorney who will handle the closing for you); never give money to the seller until the deal is closed. If the deal falls through, it's very difficult to get your money back from individuals; your closing agent will hold the money safely in escrow.

As soon as the contract is signed, the clock starts ticking on your inspection period, so you need to immediately start looking for an investor to take the deal.

## Negotiating with Another Investor

Go through your database and contact investors whose profile indicates the deal you've found is a good fit for them. Start by giving them general information: the area where the property is, a basic description (single-family, three-bedroom, two-bath, carport, etc.), and the key numbers (current value, after-repair value, and total asking price, which is the amount you've offered the seller plus your fee for assigning the contract).

Make arrangements to show the property to interested investors. Some will prefer to go look on their own; others will want you to be there. It's a good idea to schedule things so you don't have two prospective investors show up at the property at the same time.

If the deal looks good—and if you've done it the way I've explained, it will—many investors will simply accept your terms.

Some will want to negotiate, and you have to decide how far you're willing to come down on your own profit to do the deal.

Let's say that you found a vacant house in need of cosmetic repair, you tracked down the owner, and he agreed to sell the property. The market value after repairs will be $125,000. The owner agreed to a sale price of $76,000, and you estimate that the repairs will run $4,000. You offer the property to an investor for $82,000, which gives you a $6,000 profit on the deal. The investor is going to get a property worth $125,000 after he does the repairs, which means he's getting $39,000 in equity.

That's a good deal for any investor. But what if he counteroffers at $81,000? You could do that deal and still walk away with $5,000. Or you could offer to split the difference. Or you could stick to your numbers and try to find someone else who will pay your asking price.

It's entirely up to you. As long as you're making a satisfactory profit, you can do whatever you want.

Once you've reached your agreement with the other investor, you can complete the transaction one of two ways: assignment or double (simultaneous) close.

When you assign the contract, you never own the property, you simply sell your right to purchase it to someone else. Based on the feedback we get from our students, the average fee from assigning a contract is $3,000 to $5,000, and in some areas, it can be as much as $15,000. Assignments are quick, easy, you pay no closing costs, and you're never in the chain of title. The only drawback is that the person you assign the contract to will know how much you're making. If your fee is in line with averages in the area, this isn't a problem—most investors don't mind paying a reasonable fee to get a good deal they didn't have to work to find.

If your profit is going to be substantially higher than average, you may want to do a double close, where you in effect buy the property and immediately sell it to your investor. Here's how a double close works:

Two contracts are created. One shows you as the buyer, and the second shows you as the seller. Your title company or closing agent will handle the scheduling and details like this: Your new buyer (the investor) comes in to close on the contract that shows you as the seller. He brings in all the money required to complete the transaction (or arranges for the money to be electronically transmitted), and those funds are placed in escrow. The closing agent explains that the final title work will be completed and the deed recorded that afternoon, and that the buyer can come in the next morning to pick up the key.

The owner/seller comes in to close on the contract that shows you as the buyer. As with the investor, the closing agent explains that the final title work and recording of the deed will be done that afternoon, and the seller can pick up his money the next morning.

The difference between your purchase price on the first contract and your selling price on the second contract less your closing costs is your profit. You can expect to make an average of $7,000 to $15,000 on a deal like this; in some areas, your profit could be as much as $25,000. The person you sold the property to will not know how much you paid for it (until the deal is complete and the deed recorded, and then it doesn't matter), and neither the seller nor the buyer will know how much you are making. However, you will be in the chain of title, even though you will actually own the property for just a few minutes, and you will have closing costs.

It's important for you to know that not all title companies and closing agents will conduct double closings. They require an extra degree of skill, expertise, and attention to detail to make sure they are conducted in full compliance with the law. It's a good idea to check with a competent real estate attorney to determine the circumstances under which you can use this closing technique in your state. You can also network through your real estate investors club and other sources to find a title company or closing agent that handles double closings.

Which technique—assigning the contract or double closing—should you use? It's up to you, based on the specifics of the deal. What's important is that you are out there finding deals, getting them closed, and acquiring the cash you need to reach your financial goals.

One caveat on documentation: Real estate laws vary by state. Depending on the type of transaction, you may be subject to certain state-specific disclosure or reporting requirements. A consultation with a real estate attorney licensed to practice in your state will allow you to be sure your documents are complete and meet all appropriate requirements.

## The Bottom Line on Wholesaling

Wholesaling allows you to make quick cash when you don't have any. These transactions generally happen quickly, which means you can take less money per deal than you might with a more traditional sale and purchase, but you'll do less work and you'll do these deals more often—and that means more money in the long run.

Let's take a look at another technique that lets you control property without buying it when you don't have cash.

# CHAPTER 12

# Options Put
# You in Control

Lease options may well be the real estate investing strategy that is the least understood but has one of the highest profit potentials. Even better, you can invest using lease options when you don't have any cash.

Knowing how to use lease options allows you to buy nice homes in nice neighborhoods that require little or no fix-up and can generate immediate cash as well as long-term cash flow. This is the strategy you can use when an owner needs to sell but doesn't have much equity and can't afford to list the property with a Realtor because all or part of the commission would have to be paid out of pocket.

Scenarios like this are being played out in middle- and upper-income neighborhoods across the country every day: Young couples buy more house than they can afford with a low or zero down payment, and within a couple of years the marriage fails and they need to get out of the house but have no equity. Or an executive living right at or somewhat beyond his means loses his job and can no longer afford the payments on his home. Or a family was getting by until they were hit by a financial catastrophe, perhaps in the form of a medical crisis, and now their house payments are too high.

These people are all motivated sellers, but they cannot sell at a discount and allow you to do a wholesale deal because they have so little equity in their homes. Consider that any one of these sellers could have a home with a market value of $250,000, a first-mortgage balance of $235,000, and a second-mortgage or home equity loan of $12,000. If they list the house through a Realtor at a 7 percent commission and sell at market value, the commission will be $17,500. That means they'll have to come up with $14,500 plus their share of the closing costs—and if they had that kind of cash, they probably wouldn't be selling their house.

Can you help? Yes. You can solve their problem and make money for yourself at the same time.

Let's start with a few definitions:

A *lease* is an agreement by which an owner of real property (the lessor or landlord) gives the right of possession to someone else (the lessee or tenant) for a specified period of time (term) and for a specified consideration (rent) while retaining legal ownership (title).

To *purchase* is to acquire real estate by means other than descent or inheritance.

An *option* is a contract that gives the holder a right or option to buy or sell specified property such as real estate at a fixed price for a limited period.

A *lease option* is a lease under which the lessee has the right to purchase the property; generally, contracts covering rent to own agreements are lease options.

An *option to purchase* gives the optionee (buyer) the right to purchase a designated property from the optionor (seller) during a specific time period for a specified consideration (price). It is binding for the seller, but not for the buyer.

Lease option strategies allow you to gain control of a property with the right—but not the obligation—to buy it at some point in the future. And while you control the property, it can be generating cash flow for you.

## One Primary Motivation, Many Possibilities

In most situations where you will use a residential lease option strategy, the number-one motivation for the seller is debt relief. He needs to get out from under the payments, and you can make that happen.

Here's a common scenario: Julie bought her house two years ago for $165,000 with 5 percent down on a thirty-year fixed rate loan at 6 percent. Her total monthly payment (principal, interest, taxes, and insurance) is $1,240. Her mortgage balance is now $153,054 (she's paid $3,696 toward the principal), and her property is appreciating at 8 percent per year, so it's now worth $192,456. Last year she decided she wanted new furniture and a nice vacation, so she took out a home equity loan of $25,000. Now she owes a total of $178,000, and her total monthly payments are $1,500. She can afford the payments, she likes her house and furniture, she had a great vacation—and then the company she works for says they are closing the local office, and she either has to quit or move to another state.

She decides to take the new job. She calls a Realtor, who tells her that houses are staying on the market an average of seventy-five days and that the sales commission will be 7 percent. That means if she gets her asking price of $193,000, she'll have to pay a commission of $13,510, plus closing costs. After she pays off her two mortgages, she'll likely have to come up with at least $1,000 and maybe more in cash to close the deal—and while the property is on the market, she needs to make the payments. In the meantime, she's preoccupied with moving, she has virtually no savings, and she just wants to be rid of the obligation of this particular house.

*The primary motivation for sellers who accept lease option offers is debt relief.*

So she calls you because she saw your ad saying that you buy houses fast. You explain that when you buy for cash, it must be at a significant discount, and she doesn't have enough equity for that. However, you can buy with terms, and your terms are that you will lease her house for three years with an option to buy. Your lease payments will be $1,500, the same amount of her monthly payments. Your option price (the amount you'll pay for the property) is $183,000 (her asking price less a substantial portion of the Realtor commission). If she agrees, you'll put a tenant in the house on a two-year lease option (or rent to own) contract.

While you are leasing the house from her, you are making her payments, keeping her credit in good shape, and she still has all the benefits of ownership. She can treat the property as an investment and write off the expenses. You can buy the house at any time during the three-year term of the contract.

You find a tenant who wants to buy the house but has a slightly blemished credit rating and needs some time to come up with the down payment. The tenant agrees to rent the house for $1,650 per month for two years with an option to purchase the house for $215,000 at any time during that period. If the house maintains its current appreciation rate of 8 percent per year, it will have a market value of $225,115 at the end of the lease option period. That means your tenant will be able to get into the house with $10,000 in equity. You'll exercise your option to purchase the property for $183,000 at whatever point your tenant chooses to exercise his option. If the tenant goes the full term of the lease before closing on the house, you'll net $32,000 on the sale of the property (you'll do a double close, as we discussed in the previous chapter) plus $150 per month or a total of $3,600 in positive cash flow from the rent. The seller will get $183,000—but because you've been making her mortgage payments, she'll owe only $170,000 on her mortgage, so she'll walk away with $13,000 instead of having to pay to sell her house.

Did everybody win? Yes. The seller made $13,000 in cash plus had all the benefits of property ownership during the two-year term of the lease. The renter/buyer was able to live in a nice house for two years while saving up for the down payment and improving his credit so he could qualify for a loan, and then got the house at $10,000 below market value. And you made more than $35,000 on the deal.

How many of these deals would you have to do each year at $35,000 each to change your life?

## Types of Lease Option Strategies

Let's look at seven different ways you can use lease options.

First, if you don't already own your own home, use a lease option to buy a personal residence. It lets you make a smaller down payment, lock in the price, and it's easier to qualify for the mortgage when it's time to close.

Second, if you have the resources, buy a property then lease-option it to a tenant/buyer. I'll explain later on in this chapter why tenant/buyers are more desirable than traditional rental tenants.

You'll get a nonrefundable option consideration at the beginning of the lease, the tenant/buyer pays down the principal on your mortgage, you both benefit from appreciation, and if the option isn't exercised, you aren't hurt.

Third, do a sandwich lease option. This is what was described in the example about the seller who had to move out of state. You lease-option the property from the seller; you find a tenant/buyer who lease-options from you. You profit from controlling but not owning the property. Your risk and management responsibilities are minimal. Finally, you have multiple exit strategies. If your tenant/buyer does not exercise his option, you can walk away from the deal by not exercising your own option; you can assign your contract to another investor; you can find a traditional tenant; or you can buy the property yourself and put it in your portfolio.

*Lease options allow you to help buyers and sellers solve their real estate problems in a positive way.*

Fourth, if the property is distressed, consider a fixer-upper lease option. Your buyer does the rehab while you still own the property, then he exercises his option to buy and you close on the deal. You profit from a rehab without doing the work yourself, and your buyer can be either another investor or a homeowner. However, with a fixer-upper lease option, do not allow the buyer to occupy the property until the rehab work is completed.

Fifth, consider a multi-unit lease option that will let you acquire multi-unit buildings with a smaller-than-normal down payment. You'll benefit from the cash flow while improving your ability to qualify for financing. Or you can assign the deal to another investor and profit without ever owning.

Sixth, do a purchase option without a lease. This allows you to tie up a property to prevent someone else from buying it while you obtain financing or find a buyer, and allows you to take advantage of appreciating markets. This is most commonly used to purchase raw land for development, a strategy that we'll be discussing in greater detail in later chapters.

Seventh, put together a great option deal and then assign it to another investor—just as you learned how to do with wholesale deals in the preceding chapter. You'll profit from your knowledge and get paid for negotiating the deal.

## Why Would People Use Lease Options?

If you're going to effectively use lease options, you need to understand why they can be a great alternative to an outright sale or purchase.

As I explained, an owner/seller will consider a lease option if he needs to sell but doesn't have enough equity in the property to sell immediately through traditional methods. A buyer will turn to a lease option if he has flawed credit and needs some time to be able to come up with the down payment.

For both of these groups of people, the circumstances that contribute to their situations are the same: foreclosure, the need for significant debt relief, divorce, loss of job, death, illness, and other life changes. You may also find motivated sellers among other investors— perhaps an inexperienced landlord with problem tenants (because he didn't screen them properly) or one who has overextended himself with repairs and now just wants to get rid of what has become a headache. By offering lease options to these sellers and buyers, you are helping them solve their real estate problem in a positive way.

## Dealing with the Seller

If you are marketing your business properly, you will get calls from owner/sellers who are ideal candidates for a lease option. You'll be able to figure that out very early in your conversation when you start asking questions about the property. While there are always exceptions, your basic rule is that when there is little to no equity in a property, consider a lease option deal.

You can set the stage for either a wholesale or a lease option deal during the first few minutes of your conversation. Say something like this:

"Let me explain how I buy. I buy cash or terms. If I purchase your property on a cash basis, I'm going to need a significant discount. If I purchase on a terms basis, I could probably pay you closer to your asking price." Then take a brief break from discussing the deal and ask a personal question that will help you bond with the seller. You could ask what he does for a living; if you hear a child or a dog in the background, ask about them. The key is to say something that will indicate your sincere interest in the seller as an individual you might be able to help, not just as the source of a deal you can make money on.

Then bring the conversation back to the reason he called you. "As I said, I buy cash or terms. If I buy your house cash, I'm most likely going to resell it in the near future. If I purchase it on a terms basis, I'm probably going to hold it in my portfolio. Would you like to know more?"

When the seller says yes, he is giving you permission to ask enough questions to determine what kind of offer you want to make—and if you can even make an offer. When you've determined that the situation could be a workable lease option deal, say, "I hope you can appreciate the fact that we can't pay you cash for your property because you are unable to give us the discount we would need to make a profit. However, that doesn't mean we can't buy your property. One thing that may work is our lease option program, where we guarantee to make your monthly payment for an agreed-on period of time and then pay you close to your asking price. Would you be interested in hearing more about this program?"

If he says yes, set a time to meet with him at the property as soon as possible. Evaluate the property and the neighborhood, and then make your offer.

Your option price needs to be at or below current market value for a period of thirty-six to sixty months. Explain that the seller will get pretty much what he wants out of the property—he just won't get it today. And if he has little or no equity, that won't matter, because if he got his asking price today, everything would go to pay off his mortgage, real estate commissions, and closing costs. In three to five years, there will be equity in the property, and he'll make money then.

The terms of your lease will include payments that cover the owner/seller's costs—essentially, his principal, interest, taxes, and insurance. You're going to put a tenant/buyer in the property who will be paying enough rent to make these payments, and you're going to have all the money routed through an escrow service for everyone's protection.

As part of the terms of your lease, negotiate a payment delay with the seller. You don't want to start making his payments immediately; you need some time to find a tenant/buyer. You can ask for up to ninety days, but the norm is thirty days after the property is vacated.

Don't try to hide anything about what you're doing from the owner/seller. Explain it to him completely and thoroughly, and help him see how he'll benefit. Be prepared to answer all his questions. For example, he'll likely ask how he can be sure that you'll make his payments. Explain that this is your business and your reputation is built on the fact that you honor your commitments.

Also, he is protected by the lease—if you fail to pay, he has legal recourse and can take back his property. Then remind him that while you are making the payments, you're helping him build equity by paying down his debt, you're protecting his credit rating, and he's enjoying the tax benefits of property ownership.

He might question how he can be sure that the tenant you put in the house will take care of it. Again, explain that this is your business and you know how to screen tenants. Point out that the tenant won't be a traditional renter, but a tenant/buyer—someone who plans to eventually purchase the property and has a vested interest in taking care of it. Also, your lease with the seller makes you responsible for repairs and maintenance, so if there's a problem with the tenant/buyer, you'll take care of it.

For most sandwich lease options (where you rent from the seller and a tenant/buyer rents from you, and you both have options to buy), your option period needs to be longer than your tenant/buyer's option period. Ask for five years and back down to three if necessary. Your option will not include any sort of early-purchase penalty, so if you get five years and your tenant/buyer is ready to close in two, you can do it. Also include a renewal clause in your contract with the owner/seller so you can extend your option if you want to. Typically, that's a line that says, "At the end of the term of this agreement, buyer's option may be extended for a period of one year for an additional option consideration of $1,000."

The key to your success in acquiring property through lease options is building rapport with the owner/seller, making him feel like he has choices, and explaining your program so that he sees the benefits to him. Don't make the mistake of displaying an attitude that conveys a message of "You're in a tough position and you have no other choice but to give your home to me at a dirt-cheap price." Instead, make it clear that you're on his side and that you want to help him find a solution that will truly be a win for him, a win for you, and a win for the tenant/buyer.

## Making the Deal Work

These tips will help you put together profitable lease option deals with owner/sellers:

▼ Focus on desirable neighborhoods—working-, middle-, and upper-income areas. You want to get options on houses in neighborhoods where people want to buy their own homes.

▼ Get in the deal with as little cash as possible. You'll usually have to offer the owner/seller an option consideration (just as you expect to get from the tenant/buyer), but keep it low.

▼ Give yourself plenty of time. Your option period should be for as long as possible—at least three years and more if the owner/seller agrees. Delay the start of payments for at least thirty days after the property is vacant to give yourself time to find a good tenant/buyer.

▼ Check the title. Do a preliminary title search to make sure you know everything that will have to be paid when you exercise your option and purchase the property.

▼ Avoid small houses. The most popular houses have three or four bedrooms. The market for smaller houses (one and two bedrooms) or even larger ones (five or more bedrooms) is significantly narrower. By focusing on three- and four-bedroom houses, you'll keep your pool of potential tenant/buyers as large as possible.

▼ Do the paperwork in your company name. As part of your asset-protection strategy, all of the contracts should be in your company name.

▼ Be sure you have the right insurance. Your insurance policies must match the occupancy of the property, which means that once you put a tenant/buyer in the house, you need a landlord policy.

▼ Use an escrow account to make and receive payments. Do not process these funds through your personal or business bank accounts.

▼ Don't do repair and maintenance. Repair and maintenance is the responsibility of your tenant/buyer; if he fails to maintain the property, he is in violation of his lease agreement.

## Handling the Details: The Paperwork with the Owner/Seller

A lease option transaction doesn't have to be complicated, but you do need to be sure you have the right paperwork completed accurately. I'm going to give you a list of the typical documents you'll use with your owner/sellers; however, it's a good idea to check with a local real estate attorney to make sure you have all the appropriate and necessary documents required for a real estate transaction in your state.

*Property information sheet.* Create your own standard form that you can fill out on each property you consider. Start filling this out with your first telephone contact with the seller and complete it on your first visit to the property. It should include:

▼ the full name of the owner or owners

▼ complete contact information, including home phone, work phone, cell phone, fax, and e-mail

▼ address of the property

▼ address of the owners if they are not living at the property

▼ reason for sale

▼ asking price and how that figure was determined

▼ whether the property is vacant or occupied

▼ what repairs are needed

▼ details on all mortgages, including the loan amount, balance, interest rate, account number, lender's name and address, payment amount and due date, PMI, balloon payment (if applicable), and due date

▼ property information, including total square feet, number of bedrooms and bathrooms, lot size, type of construction, garage or carport, year built, name of subdivision, gate code (if applicable), taxes, homeowners association dues, and date of next payment (if applicable)

▼ insurance information, including company, agent, contact details, premium amount, policy number, and renewal date

▼ notes on tangible items in the house, including range, refrigerator, microwave, dishwasher, washer, and dryer

▼ a space for other notes

You might also want to develop a basic inspection sheet so you can make notes for yourself about the condition of the property.

*Authorization to release information.* You need to be able to communicate directly with the seller's lender and insurance company. Ask the sellers to sign this form on your first visit to the property so that you can confirm their numbers and take your initial offer to a firm contract. Use the sample on page 154 as a guide.

*Letter of instructions to the lender.* This informs the lender that payments will be made by a different entity and that payment coupons and other related materials should be sent to that entity. A sample letter is on page 155.

*Letter of instructions to the insurance company.* This is similar to the letter to the lender; a sample is on page 156. You should also request that the owner/seller have you or your company listed as an additional insured on the policy.

*Residential lease with option.* This is a basic residential lease with the option to purchase. It details the terms of your lease and the purchase option. Do not record this document in the public records unless your seller is not living up to his end of the deal; to do so may trigger a due-on-sale clause if there is one in the mortgage. This form is obtainable from various office supply resources as well as in the real estate forms software available through Wealth Intelligence Academy™.

*Memorandum of option.* This document outlines the terms of your purchase option. Record this document to prevent the owner from selling to anyone else or from further encumbering the property. This also protects your equity if the property goes into foreclosure. See page 157 for a sample form.

*Assignment of option.* This document is used to assign your option to another buyer; it's included in the real estate forms software available through Wealth Intelligence Academy.

*Addendum to lease/lease option agreement.* This is an optional document that allows changes to be made to the monthly payment based on increases in taxes, insurance, homeowners association fees, or any other assessments that are the responsibility of the homeowner. See page 158 for a sample form.

*Lead-based paint disclosure.* For houses built prior to 1978, the federal government requires that sellers and landlords disclose known lead-based paint and lead-based paint hazards. For complete information and a sample disclosure form, visit the U.S. Department of Housing and Urban Development's Web site at www.hud.gov. Your owner/seller needs to make the disclosure to you, and then you need to make the disclosure to your tenant/buyer.

When all of the documentation is completed, do the preliminary title search. Your residential lease with option should include a clause that gives you fourteen business days to inspect the property and cancel the agreement if you find any problems; get the title search done during that period.

## Finding Tenant/Buyers

There is a virtual pipeline of motivated tenant/buyers out there. They include people who are just starting out and those who have faced problems and are starting over.

Build a tenant/buyer database similar to the investor database you learned about in Chapter 11. Launch a marketing campaign with ads, signs, flyers, postcards, and networking to identify potential tenant/buyers.

If you market both sides of your business, you'll have a constant flow of properties and an equally constant flow of tenant/buyers. Your tenant/buyer marketing will be similar to your "I Buy" ads. The point is to get the word out that you have houses that people can rent to own.

*Build a database of prospective tenant/buyers and call them when you find an appropriate property.*

By building a database of prospective tenant/buyers, you have the opportunity to clarify what they want and do some prequalifying. If you have something available that fits their needs and circumstances when they call, great. Send them out to look at it. If you don't have a house that would work for them, be honest. Say, "I'm sorry, but right now

---

### Sample Ads for Signs, Flyers, and Postcards

| *General ad:* | *House-specific ad:* |
|---|---|
| Why rent when you can own? | No bank qualifying! |
| No bank qualifying! | Rent to own |
| Your job is your credit! | 3 bed/2 bath, pool |
| Many to choose from. Call now! | No-money-down available |
| (111) 987-6543 | (555) 123-9876 |
| www.yourwebsite.com | www.yourwebsite.com |

---

we don't have anything in our inventory that would work for you. May I take down some information and call you back if something becomes available?" Get their name, contact information, the basics of what they are looking for (general area, bedrooms, bathrooms), what they can afford to pay each month, and how much cash they have for the deposit. Put that information in your database and call them back when you have a property that's appropriate.

## Dealing with Tenant/Buyers

Begin your prequalifying of tenant/buyers by filling out the questionnaire on page 159. Be sure to ask for a work telephone number; if he isn't working, he can't qualify for your program.

During your conversation, explain how your program works, which is that the tenant/buyer rents the house for a period of up to two years with an option to purchase the property at the end of the lease (or sooner). You collect a nonrefundable option consideration up front (usually 3 to 5 percent of the purchase price), which is applied to the purchase price at closing. The tenant/buyer is responsible for all maintenance and repairs during the term of the lease, just as he will be when he owns the property. During the option period, the tenant/buyer will have the opportunity to take whatever steps are necessary to get into a position of being able to close on the property; those steps might include credit counseling and saving for the down payment. Explain that you have a mortgage broker (see Chapter 8 for a discussion of the mortgage brokers who should be on your Power Team) who will work with the tenant/buyer from the start to make sure they will be able to close when the time comes.

If the prospective tenant/buyer appears to be a candidate for a property you either own or have under control through a lease option, send him out to take a drive-by look at the property. Tell him if he's interested and wants to see the inside, he should call you back as soon as possible. When he does, set up a time to meet him at the property. Tell him to bring his checkbook because if he wants the house you'll accept his deposit then.

Open up the house and invite him (and his spouse and children) inside. Tell them to take their time looking at the house, and that you'll wait in the kitchen and be available to answer any questions. After they've looked around, let them tell you how much they like the house—and they will, because you're dealing only with nice houses in nice neighborhoods. Then ask them how much of a deposit they want to give you. Get at least $1,000; take the check to their bank and cash it immediately.

The deposit will be applied to their option consideration, and the remaining amount due will be collected when the paperwork is finalized. Once you have the deposit, you can do the rest of the paperwork.

# Setting the Rent and
# Purchase Price

Set the purchase price of the house either at or slightly below what you estimate the market value will be at the end of the option period. A price below market value (but still well above what you'll pay for the property) lets you make a profit and gives your tenant/buyer equity from the start.

Let's say you've got a four-bedroom, two-and-a-half-bath home in a nice neighborhood. Market value for the property today is $195,000, and the appreciation rate for the area is 11 percent. At the end of two years, the market value will be $240,000. Even if you purchased the property at market value (and I hope you never do that!), you could sell to your tenant/buyer for $230,000 and still make a substantial profit while letting him gain ownership with equity.

Your tenant/buyer may ask what you'll do if the appreciation rates do not hold at the current level. Remind him that under an option, the buyer is not obligated to perform but the seller is. So he doesn't have to buy at that price, but you have to sell if he wants to buy. And point out that it's possible the appreciation rate will increase, and if that happens, he'll get an even better deal.

So how much should you charge for rent? Traditional advice says to consider the market rents for similar properties in the area, as well as what your monthly costs are. What's more important is to consider what the mortgage payment will be after the tenant/buyer has closed on the house.

Let's say this same house is in a nice area where similar homes are renting for $1,600 to $1,700 a month. But based on your sale price and your best guess as to what interest rates might be, you estimate that the monthly payments on the house will be $1,900 to $2,000. Now, whether you own the house or have it under a lease option, let's say your monthly payment is $1,500. You could easily rent it for $1,700 and enjoy $200 a month in positive cash flow and the profit when the house sells in two years. But consider the situation from your tenant's point of view: He'll get used to a level of payments for two years that could easily jump $300 a month when he buys the house. By letting him rent for substantially less than what his payments will likely be, you could be setting him up for failure. Set your rent at a level that will cover your expenses, allow for positive cash flow, and get your tenant conditioned to the amount of the payment he's going to make after he buys the house.

## The Tenant/Buyer Paperwork

Once you've settled on the terms, it's time to do the paperwork. These are the basic documents you'll need; check with a real estate attorney to make sure they meet the requirements of your state.

*Rental application.* This document gives you the information you need to definitely qualify your tenant/buyer. It should be completely filled out, signed, and accompanied by the deposit. You can create your own application or use forms available in office supply stores. The rental application does not have to be notarized or recorded, but you should maintain it on file. See Appendix B for a sample rental application.

*Authorization to release information.* The tenant/buyer needs to sign a document that will allow you to check his credit so you can determine what he needs to do and how long it will take for him to qualify for financing on the property.

*Residential lease agreement.* This covers the rental side of your agreement with your tenant/buyer. It does not have to be notarized or recorded, and it should not make any reference to the option to purchase. You can use a form available in office supply stores or on the software available through Wealth Intelligence Academy™. Be sure your lease includes a clause requiring the tenant to pay for any and all maintenance and repairs not covered by the owner's insurance policy.

*Option to purchase real estate.* This is the document that gives the tenant/buyer the right to purchase the property for a particular price within a designated time. You can download this document from www.russwhitney.com. It does not need to be notarized, and you should not record it. Your lease agreement supersedes the option to purchase and must be adhered to or the option becomes null and void.

*Option to purchase disclosure.* This is a statement signed by you and your tenant/buyer that makes it clear that everyone understands your rent to own program. This does not have to be notarized or recorded. A sample statement is on page 160.

*Addendum to option to purchase real estate.* Use the same form that you used with the owner/seller that allows you to pass on any monthly payment increases to the tenant/buyer.

*Lead-based paint disclosure.* The same document that the owner/seller provided to you can be conveyed to the tenant/buyer.

## Do It Again

Once you have acquired a property with a lease option and then provided an opportunity for homeownership to someone who might not otherwise be able to achieve that, you'll understand that it's extremely rewarding—and not difficult. You're helping the owner/seller get rid of a problem, you're helping the tenant/buyer get a great deal on a nice home, and you're making money yourself. It's one of the best examples of the millionaire mindset in action, so do it—and then do it again.

## Sample Authorization to Release Information

_____
[name of lender]

_____
[address]

_____

Account or Loan No. _____

Borrower Name _____

Borrower SSN _____

Borrower DOB _____

Co-Borrower Name _____

Co-Borrower SSN _____

Co-Borrower DOB _____

I/We hereby authorize you to release any and all information regarding my/our loan, including loan status, payoff amount, amount of monthly payment, late charges, penalties and fees (if applicable), and any other information about my/our account that might otherwise be protected through the Right of Financial Privacy Act of 1978, Fair Credit Reporting Act, or any other federal, state, local, or lender regulations to:

Your Name, Title, and Company Name

It is requested that this information be faxed immediately to: [your fax number]

It is understood that a photocopy or facsimile of this form will also serve as authorization.

_____        _____
Borrower's Signature      Date           Co-Borrower's Signature      Date

_____        _____
Printed Name                             Printed Name

## Sample Letter of Instructions to Lender

[Date]

Lender Name
Payment Processing Department
Address
City, State, Zip

Re: Loan No. _____

_____
[property address]

We have retained a management company in [city, state] to collect the rents and make the loan payments on the above-referenced property and loan. The company is:

Your Company Name (or the escrow agent)
Address
City, State, Zip

Beginning with the payment due on [date], your check will come directly from [your company name or the escrow agent]. Please send future statements or notices requiring changes in the amount of the payment directly to them.

Thank you for your cooperation.

Sincerely,

[Name(s) of Owner(s)]
Owner

## Sample Letter of Instructions to
## Insurance Company/Agent

[Date]


Insurance Company/Agent
Address
City, State, Zip


Re: Policy Number  _____

_____
[property address]

I will be moving out of my property at the above-referenced address effective [date]. Please change my policy from a homeowner's policy to a landlord policy.

I have retained a management company to collect the rents and make all the payments on the property. Please send future statements and notices about premiums due directly to them. The company is:

Your Company Name (or the escrow agent)
Address
City, State, Zip


Thank you for your cooperation.


Sincerely,



[Name(s) of Owner(s)]
Owner

## Sample Memorandum of Option

On this date, the following parties entered into an agreement in which [your company name] acquired an option to purchase an interest in property owned by [name of owner(s)/seller(s)].

The property is described as:

_____
Address

_____        _____        _____
City                            State                         Zip

Legal Description: To be attached.

1. The term of this agreement is [insert number spelled out and as a numeric value] years, running through midnight [date the option will expire].

2. As part of this agreement, [name of owner(s)/seller(s)] agrees to not further encumber the property, nor sell any interest in the property during the term of this agreement. Any encumbrance placed on the property after this agreement is properly executed and recorded, including leases, will be subordinate to this agreement and will be extinguished by the proper execution of this contract.

3. This agreement will bind heirs, executors, administrators, successors, legal representatives, and assigns of each party to this agreement.

4. In the event of foreclosure, the owners' equity at the sale and any right of redemption shall transfer to the Optionee without further compensation and this contract shall serve as conveyance without further action.

Signed and sealed this _____ day of _____, 20_____.

X_____          X_____
[Seller's Name]                           [Your Name, Title, Company Name]

X_____          X_____
[Seller's Name]                           [Your Name, Title, Company Name]

State of _____

County of _____

The foregoing instrument was acknowledged before me this _____ day of _____, 20_____ by _____ who is/are personally known to me or who has/have produced _____ as identification.

_____
Notary                              (Seal)

My Commission Expires:

## Sample Addendum to Lease/Lease Option Agreement

Monthly payments are subject to change/increase on an annual basis due to increases in taxes, insurance, HOA, or any other easements that are the responsibility of the homeowner. The tenant/buyer will be notified in writing by certified mail with verifiable proof from the landlord/seller 30 days prior to the necessary increase. The tenant/buyer reserves the right to verify any and all changes to the monthly payment during the 30 days prior to the change. Any increase will be a dollar-for-dollar increase and the landlord/seller will not be experiencing a profit from any and all increases to the monthly payment stated in the original agreement. The purpose of this addendum is to prevent the landlord/seller from taking on any future costs that are the responsibility of the occupants.

X_____      _____
  [Seller's Name]                        Date


X_____      _____
  [Seller's Name]                        Date



X_____      _____
  [Your Name, Title, Company Name]       Date

## Tenant/Buyer Questionnaire

Name _____

Work phone _____

Home phone _____

Cell phone _____

[indicate which number is the preferred contact]

How did you hear about us? _____

Are you looking to rent or own a home? _____

What area do you want to live in? _____

Where are you living now? _____

How long have you lived there? _____

Are you renting or do you own? _____

What are you paying every month to live there? _____

How many people will be living with you? _____

Number of adults? _____ Number of children? _____

Are you currently employed? _____ How long? _____

What is your total household income? _____

How much money do you have for a down payment on your new home? _____

How much can you afford as a monthly payment to own your new home? _____

How many bedrooms do you need? _____

How soon are you looking to move? _____

## Sample Option to Purchase Disclosure

Property address: _____

I/We, the undersigned Lessee, execute this disclosure form after having read and been given (or voluntarily waived) the opportunity to seek advice as to the legal and financial implications of the attached residential lease agreement and option to purchase real estate agreement. Specifically, I/we agree and understand that this arrangement is essentially a landlord-lessee relationship, and that I/we have an option to purchase the property under the terms stated in the attached option to purchase agreement. I/We agree and understand that should I/we default on the residential lease agreement by failing to make timely payments, failing to keep the property in good repair, or any other reason, my/our option to purchase will become void. In that event I/we understand that I/we will no longer have the option to purchase the property, nor do I/we have any rights, interests or claims to it.

I/We have read the attached residential lease agreement and option to purchase real estate agreement and these documents have been thoroughly explained to me/us. Specifically, I/we agree and understand that should we fail to purchase the property for any reason, we are not entitled to any money back (except our security deposit, if all rent is paid and the property is left in good condition after I/we vacate the premises).

The landlord and/or his agent have not made any representations not contained in this disclosure or the attached residential lease agreement and option to purchase real estate agreement as to the property, its ownership, the condition, the neighborhood, or the value of the property. Lessee agrees and understands that the landlord is not acting as a real estate broker or agent in this transaction. I/We understand that the landlord may not be the titled owner, but rather may be acting as principal/owner or principal/optionee under an agreement of sale or lease option with the owner of the property, and that our estate of possession is subordinate to a master lease between the landlord and the titled owner.


_____          _____
Lessee: [print or type full name]         Lessee: [print or type full name]


_____          _____
Date                                      Date


_____
Lessor: [your name, title, company name]


_____
Date

# CHAPTER 13

# Don't Be Afraid
# to Think Big

The bigger the real estate project, the more complicated and difficult it is to do—right? Not necessarily.

It's true that some big projects are extremely complex—as are some small projects. It's not the size, it's the structure. So don't shy away from big projects because you're afraid you can't handle them. You will find that they are often as easy as small deals—or even easier.

Remember that the financial side of real estate is generally basic eighth-grade math. It's usually nothing more complicated than basic addition, subtraction, multiplication, and division—and you're allowed to use a calculator. That's a fact whether you're doing a wholesale contract on a single-family home or a multimillion-dollar commercial project.

Let's compare typical examples of a small residential property investment and a large commercial development deal.

When you purchase that single-family home, or a duplex or

even a four-plex, you will probably do everything yourself. If you do everything right—according to our strategies—you'll make money. You find the property; if it's a rehab deal, you figure out what it needs in the way of rehabbing and repairs, you estimate the costs, you negotiate the deal with the seller, you arrange for the financing, and you set up the closing. Once you own the property, you have to fix it up (either doing the work yourself or hiring sub-contractors) and then put it on the market to sell or keep it to rent it out. If you sell, you negotiate that deal; if you rent, you have to manage the property. If it's a wholesale deal, you'll get it under contract and then assign the contract to another investor. If it's a lease option deal, you'll negotiate the deal and find a tenant/buyer.

*A large commercial development deal is likely to be far less hands-on than a small residential investment.*

For an investor who knows what he's doing, it's possible to make thousands of dollars on deals that may take a couple of days' work altogether and tens of thousands of dollars on deals that take a few weeks or months. Once you do your first few deals, you'll start to feel more comfortable and confident—and safe. Many investors stop here, but if your objective is serious wealth, letting yourself get trapped in this kind of safety zone can keep you from reaching your goals.

So what's involved in a large commercial development deal as opposed to a small duplex or four-plex? A key difference is that it's likely to be far less hands-on. I've got an $80 million project in the works right now. I'm buying the land for $4 million and am in the process of deciding exactly what I'm going to build on it. To do that, I've hired an urban planner to study the market and advise me. He will study all the other projects in the area, evaluate what's selling and what the price points are, and put together a proposal of what will work on that site. Once I have that, I'll bring in a builder partner who will tell me what it's going to cost and how long it's going to take to build. Architects and engineers will do the design and create the drawings (those pretty pictures) that will be used to either presell or prelease the project—and the sales or leasing part will be handled by a real estate firm.

Most of my work on this project will be done from the comfort of my office, not driving around neighborhoods or walking through houses or slopping paint on a rehab project—although I will visit the project periodically as construction progresses. I'll put together the financing and assemble all the necessary experts to get it done. And I'll generally be able to tell you within a 10 percent margin of error exactly what my profit will be before the first shovel of dirt is turned.

Bottom line is this: For a lot less effort, I'm going to make a lot more money. And you can learn how to do this, too.

## Get in the Know with Land-Use Plans

Do you know what the growth forecasts are in your area? This information is not restricted to big developers and politicians—it's public information that you can use to guide your real estate investing strategy.

I keep land-use plan maps and a copy of the comprehensive plan of the areas where I regularly invest within arm's reach in my office. The maps show the zoning; the comprehensive plan tells me what's going to happen. The first thing I do when I'm considering a piece of property is to check the applicable comprehensive plan. That tells me what kind of development is planned over the next five to twenty years, along with other details that help me decide what I can do with a particular investment.

Every area has an economic development or a community development agency that has this information. In addition to the land-use plan, they can tell you about federal funds and other grant money that may be available to developers. For example, if an area is targeted for urban renewal, they can tell you where it is and what sort of economic incentives are being offered to attract investors and developers.

Remember, the mission of these agencies is to promote growth in their area, so when you walk in and say, "I'm an investor and I'd like some information," you'll find yourself welcomed with open arms.

*Use your economic development agency for information and support as you build your business.*

When I started this book, one of my companies, Whitney Information Network, Inc., was planning to build a new high-rise headquarters building that would house our corporate offices as well as state-of-the-art training facilities for our financial-education company.

We settled on a site in Cape Coral and I purchased the 27.6-acre parcel for $5.16 million. After we selected the site, we went to the economic development office and found out that grant money was available to do the road improvements that are necessary to provide access to the project. So we applied and were approved for a $1.5 million grant from the state of Florida to pay for road improvements that we would have done anyway. As part of our site plan, we created ten out-parcels. Out-parcels are the remaining areas of land available for development or sale after the primary user develops the site. When sold, those parcels would have paid for our land and development costs.

In the meantime, we decided that a more geographically diverse structure would better meet the company's needs, so we expanded our facilities and resources in Utah and elsewhere in Florida, scrapped the plans for the high-rise, and put the property—which we

*The 27.6-acre parcel as it was purchased and sold.*

had only owned for a few months—up for sale. Within two weeks of putting it back on the market, we had an offer for $8.5 million from the Lee County School District. My profit on that land was $3.4 million, or about $22,000 a day for each day I owned the property.

When I made the decision to put this property on the market, I knew it wouldn't take long to sell. Not only is the Cape Coral real estate market one of the hottest in the country, but the city's comprehensive plan called for the building of twenty or so new schools and the school district does not own sufficient land at present to meet the requirements of the plan.

## Investing in Land

When I started investing in real estate in the late 1970s and early 1980s, there was very little in the way of quality training available.

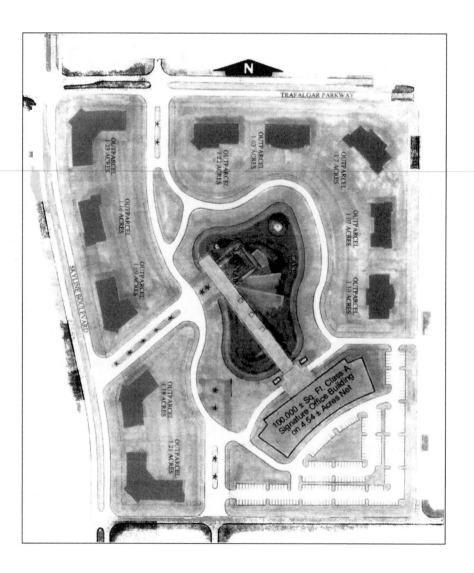

*Site plan for 27.6-acre tract showing out-parcels.*

Most of the information was in books, and it was only after I was doing it for a few years that the self-proclaimed gurus started creating book and tape packages.

Those books advised against investing in land. I had followed the other advice in those books and made money, so it didn't occur to me to question what they said about land. And the advice made sense.

# THE NEWS-PRESS

WEDNESDAY, DECEMBER 22, 2004 | PUBLISHED SINCE 1884 | news-press.com | CAPE CORAL | 50¢

**HOLIDAY STAPLE**
SEASONAL MENU SHOULD INCLUDE PECANS
■ FOOD & DINING E1

**MOM CALLS 8.6-OUNCE BABY 'GREAT BLESSING'**
■ NATION & WORLD A4

**NIAGARA FALLS MAKES CITY OF PALMS FINAL**
■ SPORTS C1

# School site sets record

### District to pay $8.5 million in Cape

**BY DAVE BREITENSTEIN**
dbreitenstein@news-
press.com

The Lee County School District is poised to shell out $308,317 per acre for vacant land in Cape Coral, the highest per-acre price Lee has ever paid.

The $8.5 million cost

also would be the largest single land purchase in district history.

The corporation selling the land to the school system stands to make a $3.34 million profit after owning the land for just five months.

At 27.6 acres, the property's size is nothing special.

What's driving up the price is its location, a prime spot at the southeast corner of Trafalgar Parkway and Skyline Boulevard in Cape Coral. Both roads are four-laned, paved thoroughfares and utilities are either on-site, nearby or on their way.

"This is in a highly populated area," Lee's long-range planner Kathy Babcock said during a site selection committee meet-

ing Tuesday. "We're trying to find property south of Pine Island Road, and there's hardly anything left."

A middle school is tentatively scheduled for the site, which is bordered by residential neighborhoods on all four quadrants of the intersection. The school would serve children living in Cape Coral and western North Fort Myers.

Lee County signed an option in mid-November with Skyline Trafalgar LLC to purchase the two adjacent parcels. That deal is only valid, though, if a pair of yet-to-be-finished independent appraisals put the market value at or above the $8.5 million.

School officials also have authorized similar

■ See **LAND** A2

**Future school land purchases**
The Lee County School District has written contracts for three more future school sites. More land is needed because Lee's enrollment continues to climb.

THE NEWS-PRESS

## LAND

■ Continued from A1

contracts for two east zone sites:
■ An 18.9-acre deal worth $1.78 million, or $94,380 per acre, for a potential elementary school at 2369 S. Olga Drive.
■ And 48 acres off Orange River Boulevard for $4.32 million, or $90,000 per acre, for a flexible site that could accommodate a high school or an elementary and middle school combination.

School board members are scheduled to ratify contracts for the Cape Coral and Olga Drive

sites on Feb. 8.

Skyline Trafalgar incorporated on May 20 and purchased the land for $5.16 million on June 22. Skyline Trafalgar partner Russ Whitney said the Whitney Education Group Inc., of which he also serves as CEO and is a partner, abandoned earlier plans to construct its 100,000-square-foot headquarters on that site. Whitney Education Group trains people in investment strategies.

According to the Florida Department of State, Division of Corporations, Skyline Trafalgar's sole manager is listed as Ron Simon, of Cape Coral, who also is one of five partners

with Whitney Education Group.

Skyline Trafalgar bought the property in May from Cape Trafalgar LLC, which lists Kurt Lacks, of Michigan, and Howard Freidin, of Fort Myers, as its managers.

Cape Coral's hot real estate market helped fuel a profit from the acquisition of $3.34 million, or more than $22,000 per day, between June and November. That is a 35 percent jump in the five months Skyline owned the land.

Whitney said Tuesday that he received other offers in the same price range, but would rather sell to the school district because it serves a public inter-

est. However, he added that simply making $400,000 worth of water and sewer improvements could have driven the price as high as $11 million for commercial interests.

Some residents can't help but be in awe of the Cape's sky-high real estate market.

Nancy Shaffer, who has lived near the Trafalgar Parkway/Skyline Boulevard intersection for 14 years, attributes the boom to a 1997 project linking central Cape with Fort Myers.

"The Midpoint Bridge started it all," Shaffer said.

Babcock sees about a dozen more contracts on the horizon

as the school district tries to build its real estate portfolio heading into a 10-year, 49-school construction plan.

That portfolio will take" a small step backward in the coming weeks as Lee sells a quarter-acre lot at 3320 S.W. 17th Place in Cape Coral that has been deemed unnecessary.

The district previously identified 248.3 acres of unused space on existing school campuses, but Superintendent James Browder said splitting off some of that land for a quick profit won't happen.

"We're land poor, so we can't afford to sell anything," Browder said.

---

Essentially, their message was that raw land is an alligator; it just sits there and eats up cash because you can't generate revenue by renting it. For most beginning investors, especially those who don't have a lot of cash, it's better to focus on properties that can produce an immediate income, such as single-family or small multi-unit properties.

That's why, for many years, I wouldn't even look at undeveloped land. And today, I don't like to think about all the opportunities I

*Article from the* Fort Myers News-Press *about land sold to the Lee County School District.*

missed—so I don't think about them. I'm just not going to miss any more. And the millionaire mindset encourages this view. Don't spend time crying over what might have been. Live and learn and move on to the next opportunity. I also don't spend time thinking about the mistakes I made or the ones I managed to avoid making. I don't dwell on the past. I take the lessons that experience provides, and I focus on the future.

So how did I figure out that there were incredible opportunities in land development? Several years ago, someone brought me a deal on a piece of undeveloped land. This person had done his homework and presented the deal to me in a way that let me clearly see the potential of this particular investment (something you need to keep in mind as you read Chapters 17 and 18, which discuss getting your deals funded). I invested in this particular deal, then started to look more closely at the opportunities in land. I used my experience and my Power Team network to dig up more information on land investments. I had already done some investing in residential lots, so I decided to research the potential in larger parcels.

I realized that there are many ways to invest in land. You can actually contract for it and sell it before you close, and make a profit—much as you learned how to do in Chapter 11 with wholesale residential properties. You can buy a large tract, break it up and sell off pieces, or have it rezoned, then sell it. Or you can develop it yourself. And if you do it right, you may even have less risk than when you buy a duplex or triplex.

There is a perception of risk when dealing with raw land that I think comes from two factors: One is that not many people do it, and the other is that the dollar amounts are usually substantial when you're dealing with large tracts. But the reality is that investing in land is actually less risky than investing in developed property, if you do it right.

Once I started to understand the potential of land, I never looked at a vacant lot the same way. I began looking through my investor eyes.

There's a piece of property not too far from my house that I have driven past almost every day for more than fifteen years. It was vacant, just sitting there, and I ignored it while going back and forth to my office for years. Shortly after I did my first few land deals, a "For Sale" sign went up on that property. It was zoned for eighteen residential units, and the asking price was $230,000 (or $12,777 per unit). I knew builders who were happily paying $20,000 to $25,000 per unit in land costs, so the profit potential was obvious. My construction company bought the land in March for $227,960 ($47,960 cash and a $180,000 loan). Within a month, I found a builder who was doing a condominium project in the area. I showed him the property, and he made an offer of $378,000 ($21,000 per unit), and we closed on the deal at the end of May, for a $150,000 profit.

Think about this: I saw the property, bought it, and sold it for a $150,000 profit in about ten weeks. I was able to do it because I was paying attention, I knew my market, and I had a solid network of contacts in place—all things people who have a millionaire real estate mindset do automatically. And this is not a once-in-a-lifetime sort of deal—it's the kind of thing I do regularly. And you can do it, too. You probably have an abundance of similar opportunities in your own area that it's just never occurred to you to check out.

## The Teacher Needed to Be Taught

Once I saw the potential in land, I made a concentrated effort to learn more about it. There weren't many people who were doing it, and certainly no one was teaching it. So I taught myself.

I talked to Realtors, I talked to brokers, I talked to other investors who were dealing in land. I read some books on land development—and the books that are out there on this subject are *not* what you would call light reading. They are very technical and very hard to read. But I learned, and now I can show others how to do it in a way that's easy to understand.

There is a serious misperception that real estate developers are only huge corporations. In fact, there are many developers who work as individuals or who put together partnerships for specific projects—and there's plenty of room in the market for more.

One of the ways I gauge the market is to listen to the questions I get from our students. They ask about the things they're either doing or want to do, things that—for the most part—their market is supporting. In the past few years, I've seen a tremendous increase in questions about land development and syndication. Syndication is simply the process of putting together the funding by assembling a group of investors, and I'll explain how to do that in Chapter 18.

Our students essentially told me that we needed to create a comprehensive training program on land development and syndication. So we did. This is an advanced training that requires a fundamental knowledge of real estate investing. When students complete this training, they'll have the tools they need to make money in land development, regardless of how much of their own cash they have available to invest.

## Vision Is Critical

As I advised in Chapter 10, learn to see things that others miss. Look at raw land and see homes, apartments, condos, or offices there. Look at underutilized property and see what it could be if you applied my higher and better use strategy.

Let me take a moment to explain that raw land and commercial properties are often priced by the square foot or by the acre. This is one of the ways that you can compare costs, because you aren't likely to have many closely comparable sales to use as a valuation tool. For example, let's say you found a quarter-acre lot zoned for commercial use and priced at $55,000. Across the street is a half-acre parcel that sold two months ago for $98,000. The price of the quarter-acre lot is $5 per square foot; the half-acre lot sold for $4.50 per square foot. The two parcels are not comparable the way two three-bedroom houses would be, but by calculating the square-foot price you can get a better feel for market values.

Here's how having vision made me $1 million: I noticed that several adjacent commercial properties with different owners were on the market in Cape Coral. One was a prime piece on the corner of a main intersection, and it was priced at $12 a square foot. The sellers of the adjoining parcels, which fronted secondary streets, were asking anywhere from $3.50 to $7 a foot.

I figured out that if I bought all the adjoining parcels, my average price for the entire purchase would be about $6.80 a square foot, and the going price in the area for low-end commercial with water and sewer was at least $10 a foot at the time. With land values skyrocketing, that property will be worth much, much more by the time you are reading this.

*Think big and don't be afraid of numbers that include a lot of zeros.*

As it stood, the owner of the prime property wanted above-market rates—not a particularly good investment by itself. But the folks with the secondary pieces were willing to sell well below market because their property didn't have much value—that is, it didn't have much value until I bought it all and connected it together. Once I owned it, I was able to sell part of it less than a year later to a major hotel chain for $12 a square foot, almost

*Adjacent commercial properties were purchased separately, then combined to increase the value.*

double the average price per square foot I paid. I put the rest of it on the market and accepted an offer of $17 a foot from a development group that wants to build professional office space. My profit was more than $1 million for some land nobody really wanted that I owned for less than a year and didn't do anything to improve.

## Add On Some Zeros

The reason I'm telling you about these deals is this: Think big and don't be afraid of numbers that include lots of zeros. Apply sound investing strategies and create safety nets through your contracts and by having multiple exit plans, and then move ahead.

Let's say you found a cosmetically distressed duplex in a middle-income neighborhood. You can buy it for $150,000, and you estimate the repairs will run about $13,000. When rehabbed, the property will appraise at $190,000, and the market rent will be $1,050 per unit, or $2,100 per month. Would you buy that property? I hope you'd jump at it, because whether you sold it for quick cash or kept it for long-term cash flow, that's a virtual can't-lose deal.

Now let's say you found a ten-acre tract of land on the market for $150,000. You can set aside two acres for common-area amenities, then break up the remaining eight acres into quarter-acre home sites and sell them for $30,000 each, or a total of $960,000. Your development costs are approximately $175,000, and it might take you several months to complete your horizontal engineering (which is the construction and/or installation of your infrastructure, such as roads, sidewalks, water, sewer, electric, and so on), permitting, and landscape architecture, and start selling the lots. Would you do that deal? If you pass it up, someone like me is going to enjoy the $635,000 profit that land will generate. Of course, I'd probably make more than that, because I'd sell at least some of the lots to my own construction company and make another profit when the house is built and sold. That, my friend, is the real estate millionaire mindset at work.

Do not avoid an opportunity like this with the excuse that you can afford to do the duplex deal but you don't have the cash for the land development deal. There are plenty of investors out there who don't have the time or interest to find deals, but who would love to put up the money for a share of the profits.

My point is: Don't be afraid of high-dollar deals. When you know what you're doing, they're easier and far more profitable than low-dollar investments.

# CHAPTER 14

# Investing in Raw Land

Most real estate investment advisors will tell you to stick to buying buildings. While that works, and it can certainly make you a millionaire, if you have a true millionaire mindset, you don't want to miss out on other real estate opportunities. Undeveloped land is just one such opportunity.

Changing demographics—in particular, the baby boom generation reaching retirement age—is driving the values of raw land in the Sunbelt up substantially. As recently as twenty years ago, investors had a saying that raw land eats, it doesn't feed. It just sits there and eats money in terms of taxes and maintenance; it generates nothing in terms of revenue. In the Sunbelt, and other areas that have become popular, things have changed.

Baby boomers are looking to retire in attractive climates. They're tired of shoveling snow and dealing with frigid winter temperatures. No matter where you live, you probably have opportunities in your backyard in the form of undeveloped land.

If you're not in an attractive climate, you still have plenty of opportunities—you just might have to look around a little harder, or a little farther, to find them.

## Who's in the Game?

One of the first things you need to do before you begin investing in land is to learn the players in your area. Pay attention to the real estate signs on the larger parcels; you'll see that there are just a few people in any given area that specialize in large land sales.

Once you're familiar with the players' names, call them up and meet them. Their phone numbers will be on their signs. Tell them you're interested in the property and you want to set up a meeting to look at it and get the particulars about it.

Use your negotiating and communication skills to build rapport with the agent and/or seller. And if you think the property has potential, you might make an offer contingent on a due-diligence period.

*To learn who the players are in your area, pay attention to the real estate signs on larger parcels of land.*

When used in the context of real estate investing, due diligence is the process of investigating the details of a potential investment. This includes verifying any claims made by the seller. When you're buying developed property, such as an apartment or office building, your due diligence includes examining the operational and financial records.

When you are buying land, there's no operational history to check out, but there are many issues you need to research. It's customary to have a period of 90 to 180 days to conduct your due diligence. You have the land under contract for an agreed-on price, but you now have time to thoroughly explore the deal before you close. You can confer with the zoning authorities, architects, engineers, and other consultants to determine the best plan for the property and if it will generate the profit you want. You need to be sure you'll be allowed to do what you want—that your efforts won't be blocked because, for example, the land is home to an endangered or threatened species of animal or plant. Be sure the engineering firm you hire has an environmental sciences department that can do this particular research for you. And if you can't accomplish what you want, you can walk away from the deal during the due-diligence period with no obligation and no risk of losing any money.

## Buy Ahead of Growth

Buying land ahead of growth is something big development companies do all the time. But an average investor can play in this game, too. The big development companies don't know anything you can't find out—and it's all perfectly legal. There are two ways to do it: Buy land that's in the path of growth or buy land and develop it, thereby creating growth.

It's fairly easy to figure out growth patterns in an area. Local governments typically take aerial photos of the entire county each year. You have the right to look at those photos; they are in the public records and available at your city or county clerk's office, or through the local property appraiser's office. Go back five or ten years, spread them out, and look at what's changed. You will be able to see the path of growth in your county, and you will be able to identify the areas where you can buy land ahead of that growth. As the growth begins to catch up, your land generally will increase in value as well.

Big developers will also create a market by developing land, rather than waiting for the market in a particular area to go up in value naturally. This is a technique I have taught for years; it's called *forced inflation of the value of the property*. When you buy a run-down property—a house or duplex or whatever—and you fix it up, you're not just *hoping* the value will go up, you are *forcing* the value up. You are in control of your own profit. So when you buy land and develop it to any degree, you are adding value and forcing appreciation.

You've seen big residential projects where a developer comes in ahead of growth, buys up anywhere from a hundred to thousands of acres, and starts building hundreds of homes. That process typically works in one of two ways. The first is that the developer brings in the roads, utilities, and amenities, then arranges for a number of builders to build the homes. The developer sells the lots to the builders, and sometimes even to individuals who may want to contract with their own builder. The developer makes money on the land; the builder makes money on the construction.

Sometimes the developer is also the builder. In that case, it's not unusual for the real money to be made in the land, not the construction, and in fact for the building process to break even or lose a little money.

In both cases, because the developer bought ahead of growth, the lot that may have cost him $5,000 can be sold for $40,000 or $50,000. So if the developer is also building, he might be making a profit of $40,000 or even $50,000 on the house and lot combined. He brought value to the land by putting in roads and amenities; the houses are almost incidental.

## The Path of Progress

So how do you identify a piece of undeveloped property that's in the path of progress—property that will have some natural appreciation due to area growth and that could also have some forced appreciation from the development that you can do?

When you do this with single-family and small multi-unit residential buildings, you study the neighborhood, examine patterns of either growth or decline, do some market research, and use that information to make a sound buying decision. This is basic real estate investing that I've been practicing myself and teaching others for more than twenty-five years. You must know your market, know the values, know the trends. You need to know the cost of whatever rehab or construction you may do. You need to be able to do the basic arithmetic to figure out if you can buy (or sell) the property for a profitable price.

This approach applies whether you're buying a run-down duplex in a low-income neighborhood, doing a lease option deal in a middle-income neighborhood, or investing in a 100-acre undeveloped tract near an interstate highway exit. The numbers might change, but the principles are the same.

*Study the area, examine patterns of growth or decline, do market research, then make a sound buying decision.*

When you're investing in residential real estate, typically you do your own research to decide if you should buy and at what price. When you're investing in land, retain an urban planner to do the research and tell you what type of development will work, the strength of the market, price points, saturation points, and all the other issues that you will need to consider when making your decision.

When you invest in undeveloped land, you want it to be in the path of relatively short-term progress. The fact is that land is a finite commodity, which means there's only a certain amount of it on this earth. When the demand for land goes up, so will the value. But the demand is not uniform around the world. Right now, the demand for land in the Sunbelt is far greater than the demand for land in less desirable states where the climate is not attractive and the economies are slow or have limited growth potential.

You can buy a piece of land anywhere and reasonably expect that at some point in the future it will increase in value. Even the most rural, inaccessible, least desirable land is worth more now than it was fifty or a hundred years ago. Does that mean you should buy such property and hold it, waiting for it to appreciate? No.

You want land that will deliver a reasonable return on investment within a reasonable amount of time. And it may be that you live in an area where such land is not available. That's fine—if you are not in a high-growth area that is ripe for development, you just need to look beyond that area for your investments. However, don't use "I'm not in a high-growth area" as your excuse for not making money. You may not be in a high-growth area, but if you have the millionaire mindset, you will either find a way to make money in your market, find another market in which to invest, or create a market that didn't previously exist—and I'll explain how to do that in this chapter. The point is, use the techniques I'm showing you and get in the game.

I invest in various countries throughout the world, although the majority of my holdings are in the United States and a substantial number are in Florida. One of the reasons I chose this area when I left New York more than twenty-five years ago was its potential for growth.

I hired an architectural and engineering firm to create a mapping program for Lee County (where I live) and four surrounding counties. The program tracks all parcels of land that are five acres or more and vacant. From my computer, I can look at a map of any of those five counties and see each parcel that might be of interest to me, and I can click on that parcel and go to the public records. From there, I can see who owns the property, what it has sold for, what it's zoned for, what the taxes are, whether it has any liens—all of the public information that applies to that particular parcel.

The program wasn't cheap, but it wasn't exorbitant, either—and it's well worth it for the time and effort it saves me. It cost me about $60,000 to create the program for five counties, or about $12,000 per county. I could have had it done for less if I had wanted to map a smaller area. The point is that from my desk I can study my markets and find out the details of potential investments—and not waste my time on properties that don't meet my basic parameters.

*The local or regional comprehensive plan will tell you when infrastructure is going to reach certain areas.*

Since I had this customized program developed, a number of new products have been introduced that will do essentially the same thing for a much lower cost. One that we have recently begun using is Win2Data, a product of First American Real Estate Solutions. When you're dealing with technology, remember that advances are occurring at a lightning-fast pace and be sure to research all your current options before making a decision.

## Comprehensive Plans

Virtually every local jurisdiction in the United States either has a comprehensive plan or is covered by a local or regional comprehensive plan. This will tell you when infrastructure is going to reach certain areas. You'll be able to see when utilities are going in, what roads will be built in every area, and when they are planned to be constructed or installed. This is public information, and all you have to do is ask for it.

Take the comprehensive plan and overlay it onto your mapping program, and you'll be able to immediately see when infrastructure and services are going to reach each parcel you've identified. For example, your mapping program has identified a ten-acre parcel of raw land that's been owned by the same person for the past fifteen years. The comprehensive plan tells you that construction on a major road immediately adjacent to that land is going to begin in two years, with municipal services to follow when the road is complete. You've just identified property in the path of progress—and you've also identified the term of the progress.

Using the comprehensive plan, I bought twenty acres without water and sewer for $1.46 a square foot. I knew from the plan that water and sewer would be coming in about eighteen months. The seller just wanted to dump the property and may not have even known what a comprehensive plan is, much less been aware of what was in it. So I paid $1.3 million for acreage that sits on four commercial corners and then did nothing. I held it for two and a half years, and right now it's under contract for $8.3 million. When it closes, my profit will be more than $7 million and the city will have done all the work.

Why would someone who owns land not know what's in the comprehensive plan that affects the property? There are many reasons. It could be for the same reason that people who own distressed property would rather sell it than fix it up themselves and raise the price—they have no interest in the process. Or it might be that a land owner is not a professional investor but rather an "accidental owner" because he inherited the property and would be relieved just to be rid of it. What I can tell you for absolute certain is that there are plenty of people out there who either don't know or don't care what's in the comprehensive plan, and they're willing to sell land today that will likely significantly increase in value within the next few years.

## Create Value by Creating a Market

You can just go with the flow and do fairly well—or you can accelerate the progress and do even better. Let's say that a ten-acre parcel would be a perfect location for a retail shopping center after a road is built. So you contact the owner and find out it's someone who inherited the property when her husband died and has absolutely no intention of doing anything with it but leaving it to her children. When you suggest that her children might be happier with cash, she's interested. So you make her an offer based on the current value of the property and that includes a due-diligence period of 90 to 180 days.

If she accepts the offer, you immediately put together a business plan covering what you intend to do with the property. An urban planner can help you with this process. During your due-diligence period, you go to your economic development agency, present them with your plan, explain that you're going to increase the tax base and help create new jobs, and you'll start building immediately if the city or county will accelerate the infrastructure into the area. The economic development agency will help you with the appropriate process, which may include going before the city or county commission and/or the planning and zoning department. They accept your plan and agree to speed up the road constructions and utilities.

You've just added substantial value to the land and created a market for the property and the area.

In the unlikely event that the government agency refuses to accept your proposal, you can renegotiate your deal with the property owner or back out of it altogether.

## The Value of Entitlements

An entitlement is a legal right to a benefit or program. In real estate, a property entitlement refers to issues such as zoning, roadway access, property tax matters, economic incentives attached to the property, permitting and other related benefits, restrictions, and designations.

In many situations, the entitlements are what will create real and immediate value for a property. And while it sounds simple, many builders just don't want to deal with the entitlement process—they want to buy land that is already entitled so they can start building and selling.

*Entitlements are what create real and immediate value for a property.*

Here's an example modeled on several deals I have done in recent years: You (or in this case, I) find a twenty-six-acre tract of land that is zoned single-family residential. The seller is asking $4 million. To build on quarter-acre lots would put your land cost alone at more than $38,000 per unit.

You get the land rezoned for multi-unit residential, and now you can put 400 condominiums on it. That takes the land cost per unit down to $10,000. You find a builder who will pay $15,000 or $20,000 per unit, quick-turn the property, and make $1 million to $2 million on the deal.

Getting land entitled takes knowledge and the willingness to get it done, and the related costs are usually not substantial, especially compared to the value the entitlements bring. It amazes me that so many builders don't want to be bothered with this part of the process, but they don't. They don't care that they could be adding that $1 million or more to their own bottom line—they're happy to let you have that money as long as you're making things easy for them.

## A Jewel of a Deal

A year ago, I bought a twenty-five-acre parcel with the intention of building thirteen ten-story condominium towers (six levels of upscale condos over two levels of parking) with a total of 416 units. I wanted a signature project, and I thought the view from the upper floors would be spectacular. We paid $3.7 million for the land and immediately began the development/building process.

Part of that process was to confirm that what I had in mind to do would work. So we rented a helicopter, and we went up in the air the equivalent of eight stories to check out the view. And it was

*Undeveloped land known as Emerald Village.*

spectacular, all right—spectacularly bad. My vision of high-rise luxury condos quickly vanished.

The parcel, known as Emerald Village, still had a lot of potential, but I wasn't interested in just another residential development. So we redesigned the site plan to do away with eleven of the thirteen towers and added coach homes and carriage homes. We put the land back on the market for $5.6 million, showed the new plan to a developer, and had an offer in a week.

Frankly, we made a mistake. We should have taken that helicopter ride before we bought the land. But it was a mistake that ended up yielding a $1.9 million profit and is a clear example of why you should have a backup plan for every deal.

## It Doesn't Need to Be for Sale

Land does not necessarily have to be on the market for you to consider buying it. In fact, some of your best buys will be parcels

*Artist's render-*
*ing of revised*
*plan for the*
*Emerald*
*Village land.*

that were not on the market and the owners hadn't even thought about selling.

When I first started my development company, I built up my land inventory by contacting people who owned vacant lots in Cape Coral. I had a Realtor who did nothing but identify parcels suitable for the kind of building I wanted to do and find the owners. I didn't care if the lots were listed for sale or not. I sent the owners a letter offering $6,000 cash with closing in thirty days. I said that if the property was listed with a Realtor, to please have that Realtor contact me; if it wasn't, please sign the bottom of this letter and return it to the title company and they'd get a check in thirty days.

It was a numbers game. I'm sure a lot of the letters went straight into the trash. Some people said thanks but no thanks. Others wanted to negotiate a higher price. And more than a few took me up on my offer. More important was that I quickly created an inventory of lots for the houses I wanted to build and sell.

My general rule is to offer a fair price but below market value when I'm approaching people who have property that isn't listed for sale. I do my homework, I know what the property is worth, and I can show the owner how I arrived at my figure. High-growth areas may require a different approach, and that's why it's important to know your market.

It will vary depending on the circumstances, but typically I'll start with an offer of about 25 percent below market value and see how they react. I call it testing their threshold of pain. I want to see if I can figure out their motivation. I should point out that this works in a buyer's market, but not a seller's market when properties are appreciating at a rapid rate, which is why you need to understand cycles and know your market.

Sometimes when you approach an owner with an offer for property that's not on the market, you're welcomed with open arms. They'd rather have the cash than the land, but for whatever reason, they just haven't been motivated to put the property on the market. So then it's just a matter of finalizing a price. And I can easily explain that my below-market offer takes into consideration the fact that they can sell without doing any marketing to unload the property or paying a Realtor's commission.

Other times, the owners are interested in selling, but—like a lot of sellers—they have an inflated idea of the value of their property. I might come up on my initial offer somewhat, but I'm not going to overpay. If the deal isn't going to be profitable, I walk away.

Then there are the owners who say they are absolutely not interested in selling—and they mean it, they're not just trying to get a better offer. You should tell these owners to keep your card and contact information in case things change. You never know when circumstances will be different.

In all cases, I work to negotiate a win-win deal. I don't want the sellers to feel I'm trying to take advantage of them, because I'm not. Also—and this is important—I'm the guy who knows how to develop the property and increase its value. The sellers either don't know how or don't want to do this. My offer is based on the fair market value of the property at the present time, not on what it's going to be worth in a couple of years after I've improved it and developed it. Most sellers see the reasonableness of an offer based on today's value, not on next year's projections.

## Know Your Exit Strategy Before You Buy

I rarely, if ever, buy a piece of property with the idea of just seeing what will happen. I have a plan for what I'm going to do to the property in terms of improvements, and I know how long I want to keep it. And then I have a backup plan in case something goes wrong with my initial plan.

For example, I might buy a parcel of raw land with the idea that I'll get it entitled and flip it to a builder. One aspect of my backup plan is the due-diligence period, which would let me back out of the deal if I can't get the entitlements I want. I'm also always prepared to do the building if I have to. So if I can't find a buyer, I know going into the deal that I have a plan to create a product that will be profitable. Of course, I'll have to put a little more effort and work into it, but I'll get my money back and make a profit.

# CHAPTER 15

# Land Development:
# From Raw Acreage
# to Big Money

An essential element in creating land value is use. How the property *is* being used and *can be* used will play a key role in determining how much someone is willing to pay for it.

By the late 1990s, I had bought and sold a number of vacant lots, made good profits on them, but still really hadn't thought much about seriously investing in big tracts of land. Then someone came to me with a deal that was more than 200 acres broken up in parcels of five, ten, and twenty acres each. One of the original developers of the city where I live was getting out of the land business and selling off their remaining inventory.

They wanted $1.6 million for the package, and I thought that was a good price and the deal had tremendous potential. I put up about half the money and brought in investors for the other half. I used an offering prospectus (a complete-disclosure document) similar to a Regulation D offering, which I'll explain in Chapter 18, to attract investors.

Then I got creative. I studied each parcel and came up with a game plan.

One of the parcels was a five-acre tract that cost us $7,000 an acre, or $35,000. Cape Coral has a lot of waterfront land, because the city was designed with a network of canals that provide access to the Gulf of Mexico. However, this particular parcel was not on any water. In general, waterfront lots are in higher demand, but there are plenty of people who want to live in Cape Coral who don't want to be on the water. Maybe they have children and feel that the water presents a safety risk. Or maybe they want to live here for the climate and other amenities but don't particularly care about boating or fishing. Whatever the reason, there is still a strong market for nonwaterfront homes.

I sat down with an architect, and we came up with the idea of taking this particular parcel, creating a park about the size of a football field in the middle of it, and breaking it up into fourteen quarter-acre home sites all the way around. So every house would back up to a beautiful, safe park.

Once I had the design, I brought a builder in. I told him that I wanted $40,000 for each lot—I didn't care what he sold the houses for. I subordinated my interest in the land, which let the builder divide the tract into lots, create some beautiful home designs, build the park, and begin selling new construction houses. Each time he sells a house, I (and my investor partners) get $40,000. Because each lot is a quarter acre, we're getting $160,000 for an acre of land that we paid $7,000 an acre for. While we didn't directly profit from the land that was used for the park, I think it's fair to say we made enough on the rest to make that investment worth doing.

The builder put up the initial money for the concept and design and to build the park. I took $35,000 and turned it into about

HOMESITE 6    HOMESITE 5    HOMESITE 4    HOMESITE 3    HOMESITE 2    HOMESITE 1

BIKE PATH

BBQ PAVILLION

HOMESITE 7    PLAYGROUND    HOMESITE 14

BBQ PAVILLION

POOL AREA

BIKE PATH

HOMESITE 8    HOMESITE 9    HOMESITE 10    HOMESITE 11    HOMESITE 12    HOMESITE 13

*Artist's rendering of the five-acre tract that was developed as the Enclave with houses surrounding a center park.*

$500,000 with virtually no risk. But the best thing about the whole deal was that I realized how easy this sort of project is to do—and I had all those other parcels left to develop.

My next project was a twenty-acre tract. I came up with some ideas on how the property could be developed, then sold the land to a construction company for $2.2 million. As it happens, I own a substantial percent of the construction company. With that sale, my investor partners and I made close to $2 million.

Then the construction company had the property entitled to build 260 carriage homes. With all the requirements in place, they were getting ready to start building when another builder offered us $6 million for the parcel. The amount the construction company had to spend on the entitlements was comparatively small, so its profit on the deal would be $2.5 million. This is another example

*Finished homes in the Enclave.*

of the fact that builders are willing to pay more for land that is entitled than land that is not.

So here's how it all worked out: I bought the twenty acres for $140,000 (about 40 percent with my money, the rest with investor money), sold it, and made close to $500,000 for myself and a little less than $1.5 million for my investors. Then the buyer, a company in which I have an interest, turned around and sold that same land, and my share of that was nearly $1 million. So I made almost $1.5 million on an investment of $70,000, I never got my hands dirty, and I did most of the planning and negotiating in my and my partners' office.

## Coming Up with the Best Idea

A critical part of profitable development is understanding and applying the concept of highest and best use. You may have some

*Twenty-acre tract that was purchased, entitled, then sold and is currently under construction.*

great ideas for land development, but you need to be sure they will work before you move forward. You do that by having an urban planner review your ideas or even help you with the initial analysis.

An urban planner has access to a vast amount of information that can help decide what the best use for a particular property is. Public and private entities are constantly doing studies related to growth and service needs. For instance, the Department of Transportation routinely does traffic counts in various areas. Other agencies do different types of studies. Local governments can usually provide a complete demographic profile of their market: who lives there, who is moving there, what they do, how old they are, how much money they make and spend, how many children they have, how many cars they have, where they work, and so on.

The challenge for you is that all of these studies and reports are not in one central location, and it may not always be easy to understand what the numbers really mean in terms of forecasting and planning.

Urban planners tap into all that statistical evidence and make sense of it. They take all of the fragments and create a grand plan that says: The highest and best use of this property would be *this* (commercial, industrial, retail, residential, high-rise, low-rise, mixed-use, whatever) because (and then they explain how they reached their conclusion).

*Urban planners tap into statistical evidence and make sense of it for you.*

## Moving Forward with Your Idea

Once the urban planner has helped you determine the highest and best use for your land, your next step is to hire a site engineer and architect to design the master development plan. You tell those professionals what you've got and what you want—for example, you've got twenty-eight acres of land and you want 100,000 square feet of class A office space with parking and as many commercial out-parcels as you can fit on the property. Or you can ask your team of experts for their best ideas for the property. They will come back with drawings to show you where the buildings will be placed and what the finished development will look like.

When you approve their work, the next step in the process is for a civil engineer to figure out what the property needs in the way of services—power, water, sewer, telephone, cable, and so on—and how you can get those services to the property and then pushed within the property to where they're needed.

Then you take everything to a design and building architect, who does the design work to build what the site planners have drawn. A key element of this part of the process is figuring out how much material will be needed, how long the project will take to build, and how much it will cost. In addition to the necessary drawings and blueprints, the architect will produce what is known as a Gantt chart, which is a critical path timeline and budget.

A Gantt chart (named after the American engineer Henry Laurence Gantt) is a chart that depicts progress in relation to time. On the horizontal line of a Gantt chart, you might depict the time of a project by month over a period of years. The vertical line lists the task categories. Specific tasks are placed in the appropriate category under the correct time period. A Gantt chart is a matrix that gives you a clear picture of a project from start to finish. Creating a Gantt chart for a project is a lot like writing a business plan, in that it forces you to think through each aspect of the project thoroughly. And because it is a graphic, it can be used to demonstrate work schedules, costs, and even resources and responsibilities. This is an excellent tool to provide investors.

## Sell at Any Time

At any step of the way, you can sell your project to another investor, developer, or construction company for far more than what you've got invested in it.

## Before You Buy

In most cases, I would never buy a tract of land without hiring an urban planner to study the property and recommend the best development ideas. At the same time, I don't hire an urban planner to look at every single property I might consider buying. We do a significant amount of work ourselves before we invest in the services of an urban planner. Here is the questionnaire we complete on every

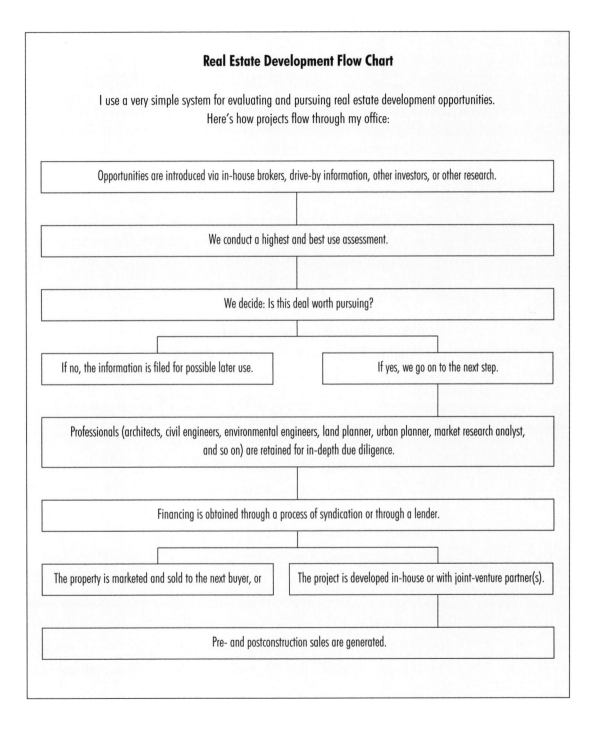

## Real Estate Development Flow Chart

I use a very simple system for evaluating and pursuing real estate development opportunities.
Here's how projects flow through my office:

Opportunities are introduced via in-house brokers, drive-by information, other investors, or other research.

We conduct a highest and best use assessment.

We decide: Is this deal worth pursuing?

If no, the information is filed for possible later use.

If yes, we go on to the next step.

Professionals (architects, civil engineers, environmental engineers, land planner, urban planner, market research analyst, and so on) are retained for in-depth due diligence.

Financing is obtained through a process of syndication or through a lender.

The property is marketed and sold to the next buyer, or

The project is developed in-house or with joint-venture partner(s).

Pre- and postconstruction sales are generated.

potential land purchase before we retain outside professionals for further due diligence:

1. Current owner information:
2. Do we have complete information about the owner(s), including specific names, relationships, and contact details?
3. Is the owner a developer?
4. When did the current owner(s) purchase the property and how much did they pay for it? (This information is available in your public records through your property appraiser or tax assessor's office.)
5. Why is the property on the market? (Why is the owner selling?)
6. How large is the property in acres?
7. What is the price per acre at the asking price?
8. What is the price per square foot at the asking price?
9. What is the geographic makeup of the property?
10. Are there any offers currently on the property? If so, do we know (or can we find out) any of the details?
11. What is the current zoning and use?
12. Is the land entitled and incorporated in the city's master plan?
13. Have the current owner(s) or previous owners completed any research on the property, including soil analysis, surveys, environmental studies, zoning, use, hazard, endangered species, or other research that may affect how the property is developed?
14. What are other real estate developers doing in the area to help us determine the value of this purchase?
15. What should we do with the property?
16. What is the projected value of the land in one, two, three, and five years?
17. Regarding financing: Is the owner(s) willing to carry any or all

of the financing? If so, at what interest rate and for how long? Will the owner(s) subordinate to the construction loan(s)— that is, if the owners are willing to carry any financing, will they allow their loan to take a second position and have the construction loan(s) as the first or senior mortgage(s)? The name of this procedure may vary by city or state, but the process is essentially the same.

18. What are the infrastructure plans in the area (roads, sewers, water, etc.)?
19. How close are utilities to the property?
20. Is there any additional land in the area for sale that is adjacent or close to the property?

## The PDP Process

Whenever a developer wants to develop a specific parcel of land, he must first present a detailed plan to the appropriate government (city or county) planners for review and approval. It's known as a PDP, an acronym for planned development project, and it must meet specific criteria and address all the issues of zoning, future land use, density, utilities, road access, and more. PDPs that alter the current zoning or future land use may require public hearings. The name of this procedure may vary by city or state, but the process is essentially the same.

Let's take a look at the PDP process and the issues you need to address.

*Current zoning.* What is the existing zoning for the parcel of land, and does it meet your future needs? Many larger parcels of land are zoned AG (agriculture). If the current zoning is different from what your plan needs, you'll need to apply for a zoning change. Communities have very specific procedures in place for zoning changes, and the planning and zoning department will tell you what to do.

*Future land use.* Most counties and cities have already determined the ideal and best use of each property within their jurisdiction. This information is contained in the county's or city's Master Plan. Regardless of the current zoning, you should review the Master Plan and, in particular, study the Future Land-Use map. If the city or county has not planned any zoning changes for the property, you can proceed with your PDP. If the Future Land-Use plan shows a new or different zoning, you need to apply for a future-land-use change, which is more difficult than an existing zoning change, because it has an impact on the city's Master Plan. This is especially true for property planned for schools, parks, fire or police stations, retail shopping, and light industrial.

*Conceptual plan.* Retain an engineering firm to prepare a conceptual plan for the property. Provide the firm with your concept for the property. The engineering firm will research the required setbacks, as well as the availability and specific location of utilities (sewer, water, electric, cable, gas, and so on), or, if utilities are not available at the property, will determine the closest access and the cost of extending the service to the property. The engineering firm will also determine the entrance and egress of major roads to the parcel. If the property is located on a major roadway, you will likely need approval from your state's Department of Transportation to egress. In addition, a survey of the property should be conducted to confirm and verify the dimensions on the plat.

*PDP submission.* When the conceptual plan is finalized, submit it to the city or county for initial review. You'll likely receive a report back that includes a list of questions or concerns that you must respond to in writing.

*Homeowners association.* If the new plan is a deed-restricted parcel, you may need to establish a homeowners association for the new residents. This process is essentially the same as creating a new corporation, with elected officers, written bylaws, and restrictions and covenants.

*Public hearing.* Once the conceptual plan is approved, notify all residents and businesses within approximately a quarter-mile radius of the parcel. They will have the opportunity to review your plan and ask questions at a city or county planning board meeting. Typically, there will be two public hearings. At this point, you can usually begin marketing the new parcels and taking reservations from prospective buyers, but you cannot process any contracts until the new lots are platted and recorded.

*Platting of new parcels.* Once the project is fully approved, the engineering firm records the new plats. If the plan calls for common areas or a recreation area, you will need to post a construction bond with the city or county to ensure that these areas will be constructed. Once the new plats are recorded, you can begin to sell and close on the new individual lots.

Each PDP request is unique, and the process can take between four months and a year, depending on the complexity of the project.

## Real Estate Development Terms

Before you get into the game, be sure you can speak the language of real estate development. Here are some of the common terms:

*Comprehensive (comp) plan:* The plan created by cities and counties that outlines growth for five to twenty years into the future. The comprehensive plan tells you where critical services such as water and sewer are going to be installed, where bridges and roads are envisioned, where parks and green belts are proposed, and which neighborhoods are targeted for revitalization.

*CPD:* A zoning acronym for commercial planned development.

*Density:* The number of units (people, residences, etc.) per unit of area.

*DO:* Development order.

*FLU:* Future land use.

*Hard costs:* In development projects, a term referring to the amount that includes total land costs, site clearance, grading and construction costs, and landscaping.

*IDC:* Interest during construction.

*Investment pool:* A group of investors who put money into a "pool" and make joint investments.

*Interest reserve:* Putting interest payments into a reserve account until they are due. Some lenders require an interest reserve, typically six months in advance.

*Land-use plan:* The plan that outlines zoning. This tells you what use properties are zoned for, such as residential, commercial, industrial, light industrial, and so on.

**Learn to speak the language of real estate development before you get into the game.**

*Ongoing soft costs:* Refers to ongoing expenses other than hard costs, such as construction management costs.

*Open escrow:* The term used to order title insurance and closing escrow services. Typically, an order to "open escrow" is done after a real estate purchase agreement has been accepted by both buyer and seller.

*PDP:* Planned development process. A filing required by local governments before construction can begin; this process includes acquiring all necessary permits and other legal requirements. The approval process can take a year or more, so businesses and developers typically file project plans up to eighteen months before they plan to break ground. Most PDPs are expensive to prepare, so these projects are usually built. Study them to get a jump on where new development is going.

*REIT:* Real estate investment trust. A corporation or trust that uses the pooled capital of many investors to purchase and manage income property and/or mortgage loans. REITs are traded on major exchanges just like stocks; they are granted special tax considerations; they pay yields in the form of dividends. However, they do not necessarily increase or decrease in value along with the broader market.

*Soft costs:* In development projects, the expenses paid for intangible items such as appraisals, credit reports, land surveys, market/feasibility studies, business plans, closing fees, and so on.

# CHAPTER 16

# Make the World
# Your Oyster:
# International Investing

Whether your business is strictly real estate investing or you diversify into other industries, don't limit yourself to operating in one country. It's easier and more profitable than ever to go global.

My initial approach to international expansion was more reactive than proactive. Through our education company, we would get inquiries from people in other countries, and if the interest seemed strong enough, we would consider the opportunity. But once we began opening training operations in other countries, it didn't take me long to realize that a more aggressive plan would be far more profitable.

Our first international operation was in Canada. Many Americans view Canada as the "fifty-first state"—after all, 90 percent of Canada's 31.7 million people live within 100 miles of the U.S. border. But when it comes to business and real estate, it's critical to remember that Canada is indeed a foreign country with its own unique culture, legal structure, and political climate. In fact, some of the provinces in Canada are so different from the others that it's almost as though they are different countries themselves.

Another point you need to keep in mind is one of the most basic rules of business, which is to test any new idea before doing a full rollout. That's especially important when you're dealing in the international marketplace.

We ran our first test in Canada in 1997 using our U.S. concept and course content. From that test, we learned that we had to adjust our program to accommodate differences in the culture, in particular as it related to marketing and sales, as well as Canadian real estate laws, logistical issues, taxes and duty on our products, and currency exchange rates—*and* we had to consider that the culture and laws are different in each of the ten Canadian provinces. Clearly, this wasn't going to be as easy as entering a new U.S. market, but it was definitely something we could do.

The following year, we hired and trained instructors, developed training materials based on the requirements of each province, tested again, and then did a full rollout. In our first full year of operating in Canada, we generated sales of $3.7 million (Canadian) and were profitable. This market has continued to be a viable and dynamic one for our company, and our Canadian students are sharing some impressive success stories about their real estate investments.

In the meantime, an increasing number of people in the United Kingdom were expressing an interest in our programs. In 2001, I went to England to research the viability of applying the investment techniques that worked so well in the United States in that market. I went out into the market, I looked at distressed properties, and I talked with real estate agents and mortgage brokers. I realized that the United Kingdom, too, was an excellent opportunity, and the people there were hungry for what we had to offer, so I established Whitney UK, Ltd.

My first step was to put together a team to research the market and design educational materials that conformed to all applicable U.K. regulations and requirements. We also customized our sales and marketing strategies. For example, in the United States, we do a lot of television advertising in the form of infomercials—something that just isn't done in the U.K. Instead, we market there through direct mail and print advertising. A key part of our strategy was to hire local people who knew the market and understood the culture; that approach improved our competitive position quickly and significantly.

We did a test in May 2002 and launched in June. Our goal for the remainder of that year was £1 million; we actually did £2.2 million, and tripled that the following year. Note that these figures are in British pounds and almost double when converted to U.S. dollars.

As we developed our U.K. operation, we decided to create a comprehensive international expansion plan. Our logic was simple: If we could realize this much success by simply reacting to market demand, how much more could we do if we were aggressive and systematic in our efforts? We opened in Ireland and Scotland in 2003, in Spain in 2004, and we're looking at a number of other countries.

In addition to teaching students in each of these countries how to profit from real estate investing in their markets, we are able to share that knowledge with students in other locations. So that means U.S.-based students have an information pipeline to foreign investing.

## That Won't Work Here

I have no idea how many times people have said, "You can't do that over here," or "That might work in the States, but it won't work here." When we were building our U.K. operation, people told us we "couldn't do" lease options there. But we figured out that people were just saying it *couldn't* be done because it *hadn't* been done. We did our research, determined how to structure lease options to meet U.K. regulations, and created a training program—and our students are doing very profitable deals using this technique.

*Just because it hasn't been done doesn't mean it can't be done.*

Other entrepreneurs who have expanded their American companies into international operations tell me they heard the same type of "it can't be done" thing. If you don't have the millionaire mindset, it's easy to believe the negativity and not move forward. But people with the millionaire mindset look for opportunities, not excuses.

This is not to say that you can expand a company or begin investing overseas without doing your homework. Research any new market completely; put together a solid strategy and know what you're doing before you actually implement your plan. But never just accept "you can't do that here" without checking it out for yourself.

## It's a New World

I don't need to tell you how fast the world is changing. Technology is advancing at a dizzying rate. We are seeing social, political, and economic changes that were unimaginable just a few years ago.

And where overseas real estate buyers used to be exclusively large institutional investors, we are seeing a growing trend of offshore-property purchases among small businesses and individuals. We are no longer bound by any particular country's borders; we can live and work virtually anywhere.

*Smaller economies can grow faster and be more dynamic than larger ones.*

Many developing countries are proving to be popular and profitable markets for savvy real estate investors. Smaller economies can grow faster and be more dynamic than larger ones, and many countries are enjoying a real estate appreciation rate that far surpasses rates in most of the United States.

## Buying Real Estate Overseas

It's common for real estate investors to want their holdings to be close by. In my early days of investing, I thought it was important to be able to visit and inspect my properties often. A key reason was that I was investing in low- to moderate-income areas. Typically, those areas are the most management-intensive type of properties, and it's hard to find a management company that will do a good job with them. Because I was regularly on-site, I was able to keep the properties well maintained and catch and correct minor issues before they turned into big problems. The process also gave me a degree of experience that was and is invaluable, even though I no longer do that type of investing.

While there is logic and value in being close to your investments, it's also true that refusing to invest outside of your own country can be a serious handicap in terms of reaching your financial goals.

Again, when you invest in real estate in a foreign country, you need to do your homework, as you would with any investment. Laws on property ownership and financing vary by country.

One of the biggest challenges you're likely to face is qualifying for a mortgage. Though it's easier in some countries than others, in general it's difficult for a foreign national to get a local mortgage. But note that I said *difficult*, not *impossible*. Financing your overseas investments may take some effort, but if the deal will be profitable, it will be worth the work involved. When obtaining local financing overseas is a problem, I often syndicate the deal and raise the necessary cash from our network of investors. In fact, most overseas investments are best financed with private syndications. Another option is to take the equity in your U.S. holdings and use that cash to fund your overseas investments.

If you're going to be an investor in someone else's deal, you need to really know and trust the other person, and you need to know what the deal really is. Don't just look at what's on paper. Always visit the property and see it with your own eyes. Be sure you understand all the costs and risks associated with the investment. In short, do your due diligence as you would with any investment, and walk away from anything that doesn't meet your requirements. There will always be another opportunity. The questionnaire in Chapter 15 that we use to evaluate potential investments is a good tool to use for overseas opportunities, as well.

While you can be an absentee owner, I don't recommend that you buy from a distance. What I mean is that it's fine to own real estate in another country and have a local company managing it for you, but you shouldn't buy the property until you've visited the country, seen the actual property, and done your due diligence. Study the trends, learn about supply and demand issues, and understand what's driving the market. Find out about zoning and building codes, as well as issues related to security of legal title and enforceability of property rights. Countries all over the world are showing steady improvement when it comes to processes related to real estate investment, but they are not all the same.

If you've decided to invest overseas, be sure you get sound legal advice in the country in which you're considering investing. You want someone who is accountable to you representing your interests. You also need to thoroughly research all relative tax issues. You need to know not only what the U.S. tax code requires, but also the tax structure of the other country.

*Don't invest overseas until you've visited the country, seen the property, and completed your due diligence.*

When evaluating the profitability of the investment, factor in travel costs. You'll need to consider the costs involved in making the actual purchase, along with the costs of visiting the property for inspections or to oversee repairs and renovations.

Most investment advisors would recommend that your overseas investments not exceed 10 to 15 percent of your total holdings as part of an overall strategy to maintain a balanced portfolio. As you develop more experience and expertise in the international marketplace, you may choose to increase or decrease that amount.

Finally, consider the impact of this investment on your estate planning. Inheritance laws can differ greatly by country, so get competent legal advice to make sure that your foreign holdings are disposed of as you wish on your death.

## Profits in Paradise

One of the most interesting investments I've ever made is in Central America. The process has been a tremendous learning experience and has taught me a lot about investing in a country with a different culture, customs, and laws.

My family and I have been vacationing in this particular area for years; it's a beautiful place, and the fishing is great. I was looking to buy something there, and a couple of people brought me projects, but I didn't see anything that fit with our business purposes and that I felt comfortable buying.

Then one of the largest title insurance companies in the United States opened up in a country where the investment opportunities had been moderately appealing—and the availability of title insurance made those opportunities much safer and, consequently, much more attractive.

When a group of investors brought me a project in that country, they got my attention. It started out as 800 acres in a good area right on the Pacific Ocean for less than $1 million. The investors had a development plan that made sense, so I initially assisted in funding approximately 20 percent of the project. I figured that even if the development project didn't work, we would still own 160 acres of land that we got at a great price, so there was really no downside to the investment.

Then the partners who brought me the original project pieced together some other parcels and turned the project into almost 2,000 acres with a plan to develop it as a resort. There was a rundown church that they renovated and turned into a beautiful boutique hotel on the water. Roads went in, a conference center was built, a four-star restaurant opened—the project really took off.

In the beginning, I was just a passive investor. The original partners were supposed to do all the work, and I was expecting to just sit back and enjoy the return on my money. And if the original partners had stuck with their original plan, that might have happened. But things don't always go the way you think they will. That's why when you put together a private placement offering or any type of offering prospectus, you have to clearly describe the risks involved in a project.

I had told a number of my friends and business associates about the development, and they had invested in it. After about a year and a half of being passive investors, we decided to purchase the project and take an active role in running it.

Because of the confidentiality clauses in the sales contract, I can't go into more detail about this deal, but the resort is a true paradise. We put several million into the hotel, and it's worth more than $4.2 million now. The land we paid $1,200 an acre for is now selling for $10,000 and up an acre. This is the country's second-largest development project, and it's continuing to grow and increase in value.

It has not been without its challenges. Without question, this project has taken more of my time and energy than I thought it would when I first invested in it. But this will be a showcase development.

## Things May Be Different Over There

In many countries, business moves at a much slower pace than it does in the United States. That frustrates me, because I'm a "let's get it done" kind of person. But I've learned that I can't rush someone in another country who is going to move at his own pace, regardless of what I want. When it comes to development, the permitting process may take longer in some countries than others. You may find that honesty, ethics, and morals are different from country to country. Certain practices that are normal and accepted in some countries may be illegal in the United States. Never break the law or do something that goes against your own principles. But decide in advance how you will deal with issues that may arise.

## Where to Find Information

One of the best sources of information to help you make decisions on investing and/or doing business overseas is the Central Intelligence Agency (CIA) Web site at www.cia.gov. On that site, you can access the CIA's *World Factbook*, which contains detailed profiles of virtually every country.

Another excellent resource is the U.S. Department of State. On its Web site, www.state.gov, you'll find information about various countries, as well as assistance with traveling and living abroad. You'll also find links to the Web sites of U.S. Embassies and Consulates; those agencies can help you connect with individuals and organizations in a particular country that can help you with your international investments or business expansion.

Of course, if you really want to learn about international finance and investing, attend the Whitney Education Group training on this topic, offered in the United States, Costa Rica, England, and Spain, or another real estate training program of its caliber. We teach our students how to operate an international business; IRS regulations and compliance; development opportunities; worldwide economic perspectives relative to international real property investment; and how to recognize, assess, and eliminate risk in international real property development. Our students get a combination of group and one-on-one time with a range of experts. And they leave fully equipped with the knowledge and skill they need to function in the international marketplace.

▼

# CHAPTER 17

# Funding Your Deals

Investing in real estate takes money. That's a reality. But it doesn't necessarily have to be a lot of money—or even *your* money.

Creative financing is a cornerstone of successful real estate investing. And the key to creative financing is knowing how to put deals together, understanding what makes lenders happy, and staying on top of trends and changes in the finance arena.

## The Realities of No-Money-Down Deals

Back in the 1980s, the big buzz in real estate was no-money-down deals. There were still plenty of assumable mortgages out there, and motivated sellers were willing to structure financing in ways that would reduce the buyers' need for out-of-pocket cash (they still are—you just need to know how to help them do it).

No-money-down and cash-back-at-closing deals still happen all the time. Is it easier to do deals when you have some cash for a down payment? Sure. But if you don't have cash and you're willing to do the work, you can find a no-money-down deal.

Before we go further, let's clarify what no-money-down means. It means that you, as the investor, do not have to put out any of your own cash to do the deal. It does not mean that cash will not be exchanged—it just won't be *your* cash.

I have always said that investing in real estate is simple but not easy. It's *simple* in that figuring out the deal is just eighth-grade math: You add up the income you expect the property to generate, subtract the expenses, and if you have money left over, you probably have a deal worth pursuing. It's *not easy* in that, especially in the beginning, deals will not drop into your lap. You have to get out there and find them. It takes effort and work. Once you're an established investor, it will get easier, but it will always take effort.

To do a no-money-down deal in most cases, you need a motivated seller who will work with you on structuring the financing. However, you can also do a no-money-down deal by pledging other assets as collateral for a loan.

## It's All in the Presentation

If you have a good real estate deal, you can find the money to finance it. Remember that lenders make money by loaning money—and if they're not making loans, they're not making money.

When you're looking for funding, be persistent and professional. Don't just try one or two traditional banks, get turned down, and then give up—that's not the millionaire mindset. Instead, do some research about your financial resources; find out where the lending institutions are; learn how they operate and what they want to accomplish; and figure out what you need to do to be a revenue-generating resource for them.

Many of today's active investors (like you) will be tomorrow's financiers. Think about what you would like to see in the way of information and documentation before you would invest in something. You'd want a solid, complete proposal that included all the facts about the investment, the variables, the contingency plans, and enough details on the background of the person managing the project to make you feel comfortable that she has the skills and experience to pull it off.

*Before approaching a funding source, put together a basic business plan for your project.*

Put together a basic business plan for each project, and make that plan the core of your loan application. Here's what your plan for a single-family or small multi-unit property should include:

- ▼ An overview of the project, which is a one-page (or shorter) description of what you're doing.
- ▼ A statement about yourself—essentially, a résumé in paragraph form that outlines the kind of work you do, what your background is, and why you are a stable and reliable person who can be trusted to repay this loan.
- ▼ Your financial statement listing your assets, liabilities, and net worth.
- ▼ Copies of your federal income-tax returns for the past two years.
- ▼ A rent roll statement for the property, including the current and projected figures for gross monthly and yearly rents and expenses, presented in a format that allows the lender to clearly see the profit potential.
- ▼ A copy of your purchase offer that has been accepted by the seller.

▼ Repair estimates, if you are applying for a rehab or construction loan.

▼ Legal description and any other general information you have about the property that will demonstrate that you have researched it thoroughly.

▼ Photos of the property.

▼ Details of other properties you own, including before and after photos, as well as details of properties you have sold and what the profits were.

If you are applying to a traditional lender, this package would be presented with your loan application form. If you are dealing with a nontraditional lender, do a cover letter stating the amount of money you are seeking.

When you are just getting started, you won't, of course, have photos and information about other properties, which is all the more reason why your package has to be sharp.

## Find a Mortgage Broker Who Wants to Work with You

A mortgage broker is a middleperson between borrowers and lenders, much as a real estate agent is a middleperson between buyers and sellers. A good mortgage broker will be a matchmaker for you and the right lender. This is why you need a solid relationship with a mortgage broker who understands what you're doing and likes working with investors. You may have to shop around for this person; not all mortgage brokers are willing to think outside the box or take creative deals to their funding sources.

A good mortgage broker knows what lenders want and will

know how to match your deal with the right lender. He'll help you put together the loan package and sometimes even assist in structuring the deal. Why does he do this? It's how he gets paid. Mortgage brokers get their commission when the loan closes—if you find a broker who wants to charge you up-front fees, walk away. Your broker should be willing to work on your behalf and get paid only when he finds you the money you need.

*A good mortgage broker knows how to match your deal with the right lender.*

If you're going to do lease options, you should find a mortgage broker who is willing to work with people who have less-than-perfect credit. This broker will be willing to help you screen your tenant/buyers and then will work with them so they can qualify for a mortgage at the end of the option period.

Be totally honest with your mortgage broker; don't try to hide anything about your own financial history or the terms of the deal. Also, be honest about what you want and need. Don't let your broker waste time looking for a loan that won't work for you.

## When Credit Card Debt Is Good

In Chapter 9, we talked about the difference between good debt and bad debt. Many people tend to take the position that credit card debt is automatically bad debt, but it's not. When you use credit cards to purchase consumer items and depreciating assets, that's bad debt. But many people literally have tens of thousands of dollars of available credit on their credit cards that could be used to kick-start their real estate investing business.

Of course, taking a cash advance on your credit card is one of the highest-priced loans you can get, so use this resource cautiously. Do all the calculations and be sure the deal will be profitable.

## Hard Money Can Be Easy

Hard money is a loan based on the property, not the personal finances, of the borrower. Typically, hard money lenders require minimal documentation other than evidence that the property will support the numbers. We have seen a trend in recent years of hard money lenders looking at the borrowers' credit rating, but these lenders are still great opportunities for investors with credit problems.

Hard money lenders will usually give you a quick response, close in one or two weeks, and offer a flexible loan structure. These loans are typically more expensive than traditional loans, with higher interest rates and closing costs, and most include a balloon payment due in a short period of time, anywhere from three months to five years.

You can find hard money lenders by checking the "Money to Lend" section of your newspaper's classified ads; networking with other investors; through your local real estate investors clubs; through your mortgage broker; and by searching for them on the Internet.

## Seller Financing

When a seller has a substantial amount of equity or owns the property outright, he may be willing to finance all or part of the deal. Receiving the money over a period of time instead of in a lump sum may reduce the seller's tax liability. Some sellers may prefer the prospect of long-term income rather than a one-shot payment. Also, because the buyer will naturally be paying interest, holding the note means the seller can make more on the transaction.

It's not uncommon for a savvy seller to write the loan contract in a way that favors him. There's nothing wrong with that, as long as you (the buyer) are getting a fair and reasonable deal. But always read the full loan contract carefully and be sure you understand and are willing to accept every provision. You may even want to have a lawyer look over the agreement before you sign it.

## Private Money

Private money sources are the people you know who have cash to invest and are willing to fund a deal you bring them. Typically, private money lenders will charge lower interest and points than hard money lenders, and are more flexible on their terms.

The deals you take to private money sources need to be win-win, reasonably safe, and generate returns higher than they can get through traditional investments. A great source of private money is from people who have established self-directed Roth IRAs; they can use the money in their account to fund your deal, and when you pay it back with interest, their income is tax-free.

When you approach a private money source, be able to explain your deal quickly and concisely. Of course, once you have their interest, you need to give them a full proposal.

Where do you find private money sources? They're everywhere. Do your networking among family, friends, your accountant, your attorney, your doctor, your dentist, your investor club, at social gatherings, on airplanes—everywhere you go, let people know that you have real estate investments they can make money on.

Be sure the entire deal is in writing and easy to understand. Include an amortization table so you can show your lender how much money he'll make (use the mortgage calculator at www.russwhitney.com). For documents, you'll need a mortgage and promissory note, property insurance, and life insurance on you to protect your investor. Once you do a deal and pay off your private investor, be ready with another deal for him to fund.

Sound simple? It is. The key is getting out there and talking to people so you can find the private funds.

## Partners

Simple partnerships are a great way to invest in real estate. You probably know more people than you realize who have cash and would like to invest in real estate, but they don't know how. They'd be happy to have a partner to do all the work and split the profits. Partners can bring either cash or credit to the table; you bring the investing expertise, and you both win.

*A partner can provide the cash or credit while you provide the investing expertise.*

One of my students told me that he mentioned to his doctor during a routine physical that he was investing in real estate and had found a great deal and was looking for a partner, and the doctor put up the cash for a fifty-fifty split of the profits. If you're shy about asking someone to partner with you, try that approach. Just tell people you've got a deal and you're looking for a partner, and if they're interested, they'll ask you if you'll take them on.

A partnership can consist of only two people, but it can also be more. I have found that smaller partnerships work best. The more people and personalities you have involved, the greater the potential for disagreements and problems.

Be sure to put your entire partnership agreement in writing. Make it very clear who is responsible for what and how the profits will be divided and paid. By putting everything in writing, you reduce the risk of a problem because of a misunderstanding, and everyone involved is protected.

When choosing partners, think carefully about the type of investment, especially if you're looking at a property you want to buy and hold. Be sure you really want a business relationship with this person that could last for ten, twenty, or even thirty years. You may want to limit your partnership deals to short-term investments and own the long-term keepers by yourself.

# CHAPTER 18

# Advanced
# Real Estate Funding

In Chapter 13, you learned that doing big real estate deals can be fairly simple and not particularly risky if you put the proper due diligence and contingency clauses in your contracts. But big deals usually mean big dollars—and where do you get the money?

That's not complicated, either. If you don't have cash, look for deals that don't require cash—for example, get a property under contract and assign the contract before you have to close. It will take only a few of these before you'll have the cash you need to do other deals. And you can do them with small single-family properties (as explained in Chapter 11) or larger commercial properties—and even raw land.

You can also bring in other investors. Most established real estate investors are willing to look at a deal someone else brings them. I very rarely find properties on my own these days; this is something I have trained others to do, so I can spend my time on more productive activities. Also, there are a number of people outside my company who routinely bring me deals. I don't invest in all of them—they have to make sense to me. But I look at all of them, and I invest in the best ones.

I often participate in projects where I bring other investors in. Sometimes I find a good deal, and I just want to do some friends a favor by giving them a share of it. This is also a good way to cultivate investors for future projects. Make your investors a lot of money, and you'll have a line of them around the block waiting to give you cash for your next project. Sometimes a deal takes more cash than I want to invest, so I put together a group of investors to get it done.

Consider trying this approach with a small deal to see how it works and to get comfortable with it. Find something you can get into for a few thousand dollars in cash, such as a single-family house, a duplex, or even a four-unit apartment building. Choose a property you don't plan to keep for more than a year. Put together a group of four or five investors who can invest $500 to $1,000 each. Decide on the terms, do the necessary paperwork and agreements, make the investment, sell the property, and give your investors their share of the profits. On the next deal, tack on a zero or two and enjoy the higher yield.

## Raising Money Through Syndications

Real estate syndications may sound complicated, but they are really nothing more than bringing together a group of investors to accomplish a common venture. Rather than you doing it alone, you put together a plan for two or more people to participate in a real estate investment. Syndications may be as simple as a two-person partnership or as complicated as a public offering.

Start with a business plan that outlines the project, assigns responsibility, and includes an operating plan for the participants. Spell out who is going to be active and who is going to be passive in the process of accomplishing the venture, as well as how and when the profits will be distributed. A business plan for a development project should include:

*Make your investors money, and they'll be lining up to give you cash for another deal.*

▼ Executive Summary. This is a brief summary, no more than one or two pages, that captures the essence of the venture.

▼ Overview of the Project. Include the market opportunity; the financial objectives of the project; the legal form of organization and ownership; the management team; the organization chart; basis for financing the project; and timetable.

▼ Marketing Plan. Detail how the project will be marketed to the end customer.

▼ Financial Plan. Include all appropriate financial information, including initial capital requirement; projected income statements and balance sheets; cash flow statements; description of sources of debt and equity financing; projected return for owners/investors.

▼ Supplemental Documents. Include any other application data, including identification of risks; tax reporting requirements; employee-related regulations; and all legal factors, including licenses, taxes, zoning, building, and reporting requirements.

## The Next Step: A Reg D Offering

For large real estate development projects, you may need to go beyond partnership agreements and raise money through a Regulation D (or Reg D) offering. This is an excellent device for raising large sums of capital when you need to appeal to investors outside your immediate frame of reference.

Under the Securities Act of 1933, any offer to sell securities (typically, a stock certificate or bond) must either be registered with the SEC or meet an exemption. Reg D provides three exemptions from the registration requirements. These exemptions are designed to make it easier and less costly for expanding small companies to raise capital from private investors. Certain real estate investment projects are essentially small businesses and qualify for this exemption. Please note—and this is important!—that being exempt from registration does *not* mean you are exempt from making full disclosure to prospective investors or that you are exempt from operating ethically and legally.

Your offering document is what you present to investors, and it should be a thorough and complete description of the project, the people involved, the risks, and the investment opportunity. Including a Gantt chart in your Reg D offering is a great way to show your investors exactly what is going to happen when, and when they can reasonably expect to see a return on their money.

Along with all of the information an investor needs to make a decision, your offering will include the actual documentation required to make the investment transaction.

Though the offering document is designed to provide investors with the information they need to make an informed decision, it also serves as protection for the syndicator, or the person raising the money. It's much like the informed-consent documents you are required to sign before having surgery—those forms give you a laundry list of horrible things that might happen to you, and by signing them, you are saying that you understand the risks and you won't hold the doctor responsible if any of those things actually happen.

In the same way, a Reg D offering document includes all of the risks associated with the investment, as well as a statement the investor signs that says he agrees to accept those risks and will hold the syndicator harmless if the investment doesn't turn out the way he thought it would.

So how do you create a Reg D offering? Most of the offerings that you'll see in land syndication are boilerplates, with just the dates, names, places, characteristics of the deal, and description of risks different from one to the next. In theory, you could just put one together on your own computer, but I don't recommend that. Even if you want to write the offering yourself, you should have a competent professional—ideally, an attorney with expertise in this area—review your documents and make sure you are in complete compliance with the rules associated with soliciting money from investors.

To find the appropriate professional assistance, you can check your telephone directory under "Attorneys—Real Estate." Call those offices and ask if they have an associate who is familiar with SEC Regulation D offerings and who can help you write and review your document. Set up introductory meetings with at least two or three prospective attorneys, then choose the one you feel is most qualified and whom you'll be most comfortable working with. You can also ask around among the investors in your area to see who is using which attorney and why.

I've always felt that the best attorneys are those who don't act like attorneys. What I mean by that is, I want an attorney who knows what he's doing, who understands real estate law and practices, and who makes sure that I'm protected—but who would never do anything to kill the deal. I've seen too many attorneys over the years who seem to feel that their mission is to make sure the deal doesn't work, or they just complicate things unnecessarily. Maybe they feel as if that's how they can justify their fees. But you want an attorney who is going to work *with* you and *for* you, and you can find that person by asking for referrals from successful investors. With that said, let me add that it's important to understand that attorneys are trained to identify potential problems and guide you to a course of action that will prevent those problems from materializing. Don't ignore their advice; find a good attorney who understands your business and let him work for you.

You can learn more about Regulation D offerings on the SEC Web site, www.sec.gov, or by doing an Internet search. You'll also find Web sites of companies that assist with the preparation of Reg D offerings; these sites have a tremendous amount of information about how the process works.

---

### Regulation D Offering Sample Table of Contents

| | |
|---|---|
| Offering Memorandum | Description of Securities |
| State Law Notices and Legends | Terms of Offering and Plan of Distribution |
| Summary of the Offering | Investor-Suitability Standards |
| Risk Factors | Fiduciary Responsibility of the Officers and Directors |
| The Business (the entity making the offering) | Legal Matters |
| Strategic Plan | Stock Certificates |
| Executive Officers | Financial Statements |
| Dilution | Exhibits (additional information that is important to a |
| Use of Proceeds | potential investor, including information about the location |
| Principal Stockholders | of the project, the operating agreement, offeree repre- |
| Executive Compensation | sentative statement, offeree qualification form, |
| Relationships and Related-Party Transactions | subscription agreement, and legal opinion) |

## Being—or Approaching—a Passive Investor

As you establish your reputation as a real estate investor, you will have people bringing you deals—sometimes in the form of a partnership agreement, other times as a Reg D offering. This is a good thing.

While I enjoy the actual process of real estate investing, there are times when I like to put some money into a solid investment and not have to worry about managing the details. You, too, will likely want to be a passive investor in some cases. But don't just toss some money at a deal because it's pitched to you with a flashy presentation. Do your due diligence.

Check out the manager and general partner. Have they ever done anything like this before? What's their track record? You don't want to fund a multimillion-dollar deal for someone with absolutely no experience. Sure, everybody has to start somewhere, and I'm not saying to never help a new investor. In fact, I believe in helping new investors, and I'm proud to have seeded many real estate fortunes. But it's one thing to put up $5,000 or $10,000 in cash for a deal brought to you by an inexperienced investor, and it's something altogether different to put up $250,000 or $500,000 for a deal from the same inexperienced investor.

If the investor who is bringing the deal to you has limited practical real estate experience, find out why they believe they can be successful. They may be one of my students who has received excellent training but just needs a little cash to get the deal done. Typically, this type of investor is going to approach someone he knows—and because you know the person, you'll have a sense of whether or not he can pull the deal together.

*Funding a real estate deal through syndication is a great way to do projects you don't have the cash to do by yourself.*

Keep in mind that the passive investors with megabucks out there rarely got rich by winning the lottery. They are generally intelligent, intuitive, reasonable businesspeople who made their money with prudent investments. This is the same approach you should take when investing your own money or looking for investors for your projects.

When you are approaching investors, be sure they can afford to lose their investment. Certainly, if you follow my advice, your deals will be profitable—but things can always happen to delay the profits. You want an investor who understands what he's getting into—not one who is going to be on the phone every month asking where his profits are.

Also, if you're looking for a passive investor, be sure you approach people who are willing to be passive. In most cases, I don't want an investor who wants to be involved in managing the operation; I already have a team of experienced people to do that. So unless the investor brings something to the table that fills a gap in your management or operating team, be sure he understands that his role is to simply put up the money and wait for the returns.

## Some General Thoughts on Syndicating

Funding a real estate deal through syndication is a great way to do projects you don't have the cash to do by yourself. I support syndication as both a wealth-building and cash-management tool. However, even though I create and participate in syndicates regularly, when I syndicate I want as few partners as I can get. It's much easier to bring two minds together than it is three. And easier to bring three together than it is four. And four than it is five. So my general rule is the fewer the better.

Also, it's better to make the entity more simple than complicated. A simple LLC (limited liability company) with a basic operating agreement is always better than a more difficult and complicated structure. Even if you're doing a Reg D offering, keep it as simple as possible.

An LLC is one of four basic business legal structures; the other three are a sole proprietorship, a partnership, and a corporation. The legal structure has nothing to do with how the company will operate; it defines the ownership of the entity.

A sole proprietorship is the simplest and easiest form of business ownership. The business and the owner are one and the same, and share the same liabilities and benefits of the business. When the owner dies, the business ceases to exist. A partnership is an association of two or more people, and may be set up as a general partnership (where each partner shares in the responsibility and liability of the operation) or limited (where certain partners may limit their liability if they are not actively involved in the management of the operation). A corporation is a separate legal entity that is owned by shareholders and can own property, incur debt, and is recognized by the Internal Revenue Service.

The LLC business structure combines many of the protections of a corporation with the tax benefits of a partnership. Laws regarding LLCs vary by state, but they are generally easy to form and are an excellent vehicle for real estate projects that will have a limited life span. For example, if you are doing a development project that you expect to take five years to complete and sell out, you need more liability protection than a partnership provides, but you don't need to operate under a corporation that will remain "alive" until it is dissolved. An LLC is an ideal legal structure for many real estate investments.

## Get the Government to Help

It's not necessary for you to come up with all the cash (either your-self or with investors) or find loans sufficient to fund a project. There is plenty of government money out there that you can use if the project is appropriate—and all you have to do is ask for it.

Every day, governments all over the country offer incentives to businesses to locate in their area, stay in their area, or expand in their area. Those incentives range from low-interest loans to tax breaks to outright grants—money that never has to be paid back. You see the headlines all the time: "City Offers $15 Million in Tax Savings to Downtown Development Pro-ject" or "County's Incentive Package for XYZ Company to Relocate Here Tops $25 Million." What you don't see are headlines about the smaller incentive packages that govern-ments hand out every day to attract and retain growth and development.

*Get your share of the incentive packages governments are handing out every day to attract and retain growth and development.*

Whether you're doing a real estate project or some other type of business, you are probably eligible for some type of govern-ment incentives. The fastest and easiest way to find out what's available is to go to your local economic development agency, explain what you want to do, and ask what programs are available and what you have to do to qualify.

Stay focused on the benefits to the community that will come from your project. Talk about how the tax base will be enhanced, about how many jobs you'll create or bring to the area—or even how many jobs you will *keep* in the area. There was a point last year when I was considering moving our headquarters out of Cape Coral, and the city was quick to offer incentives to keep us there.

We were quick to negotiate—and we weren't shy about pointing out what other areas were offering us as incentives to move.

When you create new jobs, you may find the government will pay you for hiring and training new employees and even retraining current employees to assure that they will continue to be employed. When you are increasing the long-term tax revenue the city or county will receive, you're likely to get a break on your own taxes.

You don't have to be the person or company doing the hiring. If, for example, you want to do some commercial development, you can work with the government to provide incentives to the companies who either buy or rent your commercial space.

I make it a point to know what my business means to the local economy. I know how much money my employees earn—and then spend—on housing, food, transportation, and other things. I know what my companies pay in local and state taxes. I know the economic impact of the students who come to Cape Coral for training—the number of hotel nights they buy, the money they spend on food and local entertainment while they're here, and the impact of any real estate investing they might do in the area.

Whitney Education Group alone (without adding in the employees from other local companies of which I have a total or partial ownership) is one of Cape Coral's largest employers. But even small companies with just a few employees, or small developers with projects that will never make the headlines, are eligible for plenty of government assistance.

Downtown areas in older cities and towns across the country have an abundance of revitalization funds available, ranging from low-interest loans to outright grants to improve property in targeted areas. Your local economic development agency can help you figure out what's available and how to get it.

Many areas also have programs offering down-payment assistance to first-time and/or low-income home buyers. Get the details on these programs—not for yourself, but for the people you want to sell property to. When you buy houses to fix up and quick-turn to a homeowner, you can expand your potential market of buyers tremendously if you can help them get into the property with little or no money down. The local housing authority can give you the information or let you know whom to contact.

## If You Have a Good Deal, Money Is Easy to Find

I own half of a seventeen-story office building in downtown Orlando, and the investor who brought me the deal and owns the other half didn't have a dime in it.

Here's what happened: The building is on land the original owners leased from someone in New York. For years, the building was one of the most prominent office towers in Orlando, but then the original owners let the building go into disrepair and defaulted on the land lease. Tenants started moving out. The big law firms wanted to be in classier buildings with more amenities. Some of the government agencies that had been housed there moved into the new courthouse complex when it opened. The investor in New York who owned the land didn't want to foreclose, because that meant he would have to take the building over, and it needed about $8 million in repairs.

An investor I know who is active in the commercial real estate market in downtown Orlando was aware of what was happening. He put together a partnership, raised $750,000, bought the land lease from the guy in New York, and started the foreclosure process.

*Renovated
Orlando office
tower that has
been condo-
miniumized.*

After all the legal maneuvering, my friend and his partners became the owners of a seventeen-story office building within two blocks of the Orange County Courthouse in downtown Orlando for just $750,000.

Of course, the building needed extensive renovation, but my friend assumed borrowing the money for that would not be a problem. He went to a bank, applied for an $8 million loan, got the first $2 million and a verbal commitment for the balance of $6 million, and began the renovations.

Loans of this size and nature are typically made in increments. Essentially, you borrow what you need as you go, and the lender checks to make sure you're really doing the work so their collateral is protected. But when my friend went to take his second draw, the bank refused to lend him any more money. Somehow the loan officer had found out that he personally didn't have any money in the deal, and that's the sort of thing that scares bankers. It didn't matter to the bank that he had brought together the investors or that he had a great plan for the building or that he had the experience, resources, and connections to make it all happen. The bank said he had to come up with $2 million or they would not lend him the balance of the money and would foreclose on him for the amount of the initial draw.

So he brought the deal to me. I flew up to Orlando, looked at the building, met with the contractors, and sat down with the banker. He wasn't going to budge from his position. But the numbers still looked good to me.

The partnership asked me to invest the $2 million and qualify (meaning to use my credit rating) an $8 million loan, which meant the building would have $10 million invested in it. But once it was renovated and leased, it would appraise at $17 million. Only half-leased, it would still appraise for at least $14 million. So $2 million cash would create equity of a minimum of $4 million and a maximum of $7 million. And fully leased, the building would generate $1million a year in net positive cash flow.

So I told them I'd put up the $2 million, but I wanted 50 percent of the building and 50 percent of the cash flow.

Now, you could look at this and think I was being greedy. If the original investor had borrowed the money, he probably could have gotten it for well under 10 percent. But that was the point: He couldn't borrow the money. And his existing investors not only didn't have it, but what they had put into the deal was at risk.

The investor who brought me the deal had absolutely no cash invested in this building. He had time, effort, and knowledge, of course—but no cash. But because he put the deal together and brought it to me, he'll own half of a building, his share of the equity will be somewhere between $2 million and $3.5 million, and he'll get $500,000 a year in positive cash flow.

Who made the better deal here? We're getting the same benefits, but he put up nothing and I put up $2 million plus the credit to qualify the loan.

And the building is absolutely beautiful now. That's not just my opinion. Someone—we have no idea who—wrote to the *Orlando Sentinel* commenting that we had turned the building from one of the ugliest to the most beautiful in downtown Orlando.

When the renovations were nearing completion, we realized that we had a more profitable alternative to our original plan of leasing the building. In the Orlando market, we saw a significant increase in office condominiums, so we decided to condominiumize the building. Instead of renting it or selling it in its entirety, we are selling the building in floors or fractions of floors. We've created a condo association that will be responsible for the common areas (elevators, stairwells, hallways, restrooms, lobby, parking lot, etc.), and the owners will pay association fees based on their space.

Because this building was renovated rather than new construction, our cost basis is about 25 to 30 percent less than the new buildings in the market, so we can sell comparable space for less. We expect to realize a total profit of about $20 million in a period of four to six months, as opposed to the eight to ten years the original plan would have taken to generate that same return.

## The Best Way to Find Investors

The best way to find new investors is to satisfy the ones you have. You can advertise for investors and you may get some interest, but there are some restrictions on that type of advertising, especially if you're doing a Reg D offering. The absolute best way to find investors is through networking and word of mouth. When someone does a deal with you and makes money, he won't keep that to himself. He'll tell people—he'll become your evangelist.

*The best way to find new investors is to satisfy the ones you have.*

Everybody who has ever invested in one of my projects has made money and wants to do more deals with me. In fact, I don't have to go looking for investors for my big projects—they're calling me, asking what I've got and how they can get involved.

Start small and deliver. Then move up to bigger deals.

# CHAPTER 19

# Getting Started
When You Have Cash

W e've talked a lot about strategies to use if you have little or no cash and you want to get started in real estate investing—but what if you have money? We see plenty of students coming through our programs—professionals such as doctors and lawyers, people who have taken early retirement from a large company and have a substantial nest egg, people who have inherited money, and so on—who have cash and want to invest in real estate, but also want to be sure they do it right.

One of my students told me about a situation where she was trying to explain to a relative—an adult nephew—about the strategies and techniques we teach. Her nephew said that he thought the best way to invest in real estate would be if you had enough money to pay cash for property, and then you could just sit back and enjoy the rent revenue.

That's not necessarily the smartest approach. Let's look at another option.

Let's say you have $200,000 to invest—it may have come from

an inheritance, a settlement of some sort, savings, it doesn't matter. But you have $200,000. You buy two single-family houses for $100,000 each and pay cash. You can rent each house for $900 a month. In the best-case scenario, if you have no vacancies and no repairs and even if you're raising the rent every year or two, you're still going to have to pay taxes, and it's still going to take you more than nine years to break even.

Now, let's say there are plenty of those $100,000 houses available. But instead of paying cash for two of them, you bought ten with 20 percent down each and financed the remaining $80,000 on each house for thirty years. Your payments are $700 a month. With ten units, you're making $24,000 a year in positive cash flow, the rent is paying down the mortgages, and your properties are appreciating in value.

Let's look at what you'll have in terms of net worth at the end of ten years. If you bought two of those houses and they both appreciated at a steady 10 percent per year, after a decade you would have property worth $518,747 with no debt. If you had ten of those houses with the same steady 10 percent annual appreciation, your property would be worth $2.6 million, and your debt would be $678,000, which is a net worth of just under $2 million.

Which is the smarter way to use your $200,000?

Without question, it's much easier to invest in real estate when you have cash, but you need a solid strategy and you need to use that cash wisely. My own personal policy is to never put up more of my own cash than is necessary to make the deal work.

## Make Yourself Attractive to Investors

Having at least some of your own money will make you more attractive to potential investors than if you have nothing in the deal. Look at it from their perspective: You go to a private money investor with a deal that needs $300,000 to close. The deal looks great on paper, but you have no money in it, so if it doesn't work out, you don't lose any cash.

Instead, let's say it needs $300,000 to close and you're putting up $50,000 and offering it to your private money investor for $250,000. If it doesn't work, the investor stands to lose much more than you, but you're still on the hook for a meaningful sum, which increases the comfort level of your investor.

*It's much easier to invest in real estate when you have cash—but use that cash wisely.*

Of course, in both cases, the investor is protected by the collateral (the property), so will a private money investor buy into the first deal? Sure, if you've done your homework and presented the deal properly. But will he feel safer with the second scenario? Undoubtedly.

## Where's Your Money?

When considering how much cash you have, look beyond the balance in your bank account. You may have more resources than you realize.

For example, do you have an IRA (individual retirement account)? If it is self-directed, you may be able to use those funds for real estate investments. There are rules and guidelines you must follow, so be sure you have a custodian who understands the details of using IRA funds to invest in real estate. If your current account is not self-directed, you should be able to roll it into one that will better serve your needs.

Do you own an insurance policy with cash value? You may be able to borrow a significant portion of the cash value of the policy. Keep in mind that the death benefit for your beneficiaries will be reduced if there is a loan outstanding against the policy, so use this resource cautiously.

Look around your home, especially in the attic, basement, or other storage places. Do you have items of value that you are not using that could be sold for cash? Maybe you inherited something like your grandfather's stamp collection and you've just got it packed away in a box in the back of a closet; consider having it appraised and selling it.

And speaking of your home: If you own your home, this may be the fastest and easiest way to get start-up cash for your real estate investment business.

## The Equity in Your Home

Consider using the equity in your own home to purchase investment property. When you do this, of course, you are putting your home on the line. But if you invest using the sound, proven techniques I teach, this can be a great way to kick-start your real estate investing business.

There are two basic ways to use your home equity. One is to take out a second mortgage or obtain a home equity line of credit (essentially the same thing) and use that cash for your investments. The other is to pledge the equity in your home as collateral for the down payment or for part of the mortgage on the investment property.

Be sure the property you're buying will generate enough positive cash flow to handle any debt service you create. For example, let's say you take out a second mortgage of $20,000 to use as a down payment on a four-unit building. The terms on the second mortgage are 7.5 percent for eight years, and your payments are

$278 a month. The property you're buying needs to generate enough income from rents to cover that payment, as well as the first-mortgage payment on the property, taxes, and expenses—and still have something left over for profit.

Is it possible? Sure. Let's say the sale price of the building was $200,000, and it has two one-bedroom apartments and two two-bedroom, two-bath units. You put your $20,000 from your home equity loan down and finance the remaining $180,000 at 6 percent for thirty years. Your monthly principal and interest payments on that loan will be $1,079. Your other expenses (taxes, insurance, water, sewer, waste collection, other utilities, maintenance and repairs, vacancy allowance) will run about $1,000 a month. Add in the $278 payment on the home equity loan, and that means you need about $2,350 a month in revenue to break even.

*Consider using the equity in your own home to purchase investment property.*

If you rent the one-bedroom units for $650 a month and the two-bedroom units for $800 a month, that generates $2,900 per month, which means your positive cash flow (or profit) is $550 a month, or $6,600 a year.

Let's take this same example from a different perspective. Let's say this same four-unit building needs some improvements. You buy it for $165,000 and put $12,000 down and spend $8,000 doing cleanup and fix-up. When you're finished, the building is worth $200,000. If you finance the first mortgage of $153,000 on the same terms (6 percent for thirty years), your monthly payments will be $917. If the rest of the numbers are the same, you'll break even with $2,200 a month in revenue—but you have gained $35,000 in equity that you can use to repay your second mortgage (by taking out a second mortgage on the investment property) or to invest in other properties.

## Make Your Money Perform

Regardless of where you get your start-up cash, be sure you make it perform. Understand your cash on cash return, set your goals, and work to achieve them.

Your cash on cash return is the return you get for the cash you invested. For example, when you put money into a savings account at a bank, the banks pays you interest. The annual interest rate is

*Your cash on cash return is what you make on the cash you invested.*

your cash on cash ratio. Let's say you have a property worth $150,000 that you were able to buy for $15,000 cash down, and you financed the remainder. If your net cash flow is $3,000 per year, your cash on cash return is 20 percent ($3,000 ÷ $15,000).

You also want to pay close attention to your overall annual return on investment (ROI). To understand this, you need to calculate your cash on cash return plus your appreciation, equity buildup, and tax reduction. Appreciation is, as you know, the amount the property increases in value. Equity buildup is the amount by which the principal balance of your mortgage is reduced as you make mortgage payments. You can reduce your tax liability by deducting depreciation and other expenses related to operating the property.

Let's consider this example: You buy a ten-unit building for $1 million and put 10 percent, or $100,000, down, and finance the remainder on a thirty-year note. The building is fully rented at $1,600 per month per unit. Your monthly expenses (mortgage payment, taxes, insurance, maintenance, and so on) total $10,000. Your net operating profit per month is $6,000 ($16,000 − $10,000). The appreciation rate is 9 percent. So, at the end of the first year, here's what you have:

Net operating profit (net cash flow):     $72,000
Appreciation:                              $90,000
Equity buildup:                             $8,300
Tax savings from depreciation:              $6,800
**Total:**                                **$177,100**

The total return on investment after one year on this deal is 177 percent ($177,100 ÷ $100,000). Of course, you don't realize the cash on appreciation and equity buildup until you either sell or refinance, but the return is still there.

When I first started investing, I set a goal of 100 percent ROI and consistently achieved or exceeded it. It's not difficult; it's just a matter of paying attention to the numbers and making sure the deal works.

# PART 3

# Beyond Real Estate Investing

▼

# CHAPTER 20

# Get Involved
# and Give Back

For myself, and for most of the successful people I know, the best thing about having money is not what you can buy for yourself but what you can do for others. Making money is far more satisfying when you have a purpose that's bigger than the dollars.

The late Danny Thomas, who received the Congressional Medal of Honor for his work in establishing the St. Jude's Children's Research Hospital, once said, "Success in life has nothing to do with what you gain in life or accomplish for yourself. It's what you do for others."

The Old Testament tells us to tithe—that is, to offer to God the first tenth of whatever God gives us. The Bible tells us that if we honor God and serve Him, we will be blessed beyond measure. One of the ways we honor and serve is by helping others less fortunate. In another scripture, we are told, "From everyone who has been given much, much will be demanded; and from the one who has been entrusted with much, much more will be asked."

So many of the "get-rich gurus" who have come and gone over the years focus on the material benefits of having money: big houses, fancy cars, boats, jewelry, and—of course—always being surrounded by attractive people. My students tend to be of a higher caliber. They're not as interested in the superficial side of wealth as they are in having the resources to make a difference in the world. They want to make a difference by being better parents and spouses and spending time with their families, by being more active in their communities, and by having the time and money to contribute to worthy causes.

## You Need a Plan

You know how important it is to have a plan for your business. It is equally important to have a plan for your philanthropies.

The more you give, the more you will be asked to give. Without a plan and purpose, your contributions may not be as effective as you'd like.

Your plan is more than just how much money you're going to throw at a problem. Yes, financial contributions are important— but they're not enough. Effective community involvement goes way beyond writing checks. It includes giving your time and influence, and perhaps even some in-kind donations (noncash gifts).

## What's Your Mission?

Choose an issue or a purpose that's important to you and focus on it. My issue is helping at-risk kids, and by concentrating my resources (my own money and the connections I have) on that issue, I make a difference in the lives of youngsters who need some help getting

and staying on the right track. I often get asked to contribute to other causes that are very worthwhile, and
depending on what it is, I either say no or make a modest
donation. Even millionaires do not have infinite resources. I
can't fix every problem in the world by myself, but I want to
make sure that I make a difference, so I don't dilute my efforts.

*Wealth gives you
the resources to
make a difference
in the world.*

Most other wealthy people take a similar approach. For example,
the mission of the Bill and Melinda Gates Foundation is global
health and learning. That foundation gives away billions of dollars, but they'd probably turn down a request to fund a local pet-
rescue group. On the other hand, that same local pet-rescue group
stands a pretty good chance of getting help from the Doris Day
Animal Foundation. Both foundations are very effective because
they are focused. I formed The Whitney Foundation, Inc., to help
at-risk youngsters. We often get requests for assistance that don't
meet our mission, and it's hard to turn them down, but we have to
because if we lose our focus, we'll lose our effectiveness.

Whether you create a foundation or just make personal contributions, you need a mission so that your efforts can have an impact.
And on a practical note, if you create a foundation and want to be
considered for tax-exempt status with the IRS, you'll need a clear
mission statement for your application, and you'll need to operate
in accordance with that mission statement.

## Publicity Is *Not* Self-Serving

I have never been one to talk a lot about the donations I make, but
the fact is that publicizing what you do for the community can be
very beneficial to the people and organizations you want to help.
We sometimes issue news releases when we make significant char-

*Choose an issue that's important to you and focus on it so your efforts will have an impact.*

itable contributions, either through the foundation or from the company. Certainly, it's good publicity for the company, but more important is that it's great exposure for the charity. It's another chance for the charity to get in the spotlight and gain support. Whenever I make a donation, I encourage others to follow my example.

If you have the resources—whether it's a celebrity name or money or whatever—to bring attention to a cause you support, you should do it.

## Beyond Organized Giving

While I give generously to my church and to organized nonprofit agencies, I also enjoy making private and anonymous gifts to people who would never ask for my help and are totally surprised to receive it.

One way I do this is to leave generous tips. I have left a $100 tip for a check that was just $15, because the service was excellent and I wanted to do something that would make a difference in the server's day. I know how hard people in service positions work, and I think they should be rewarded for a job well done. While you're building your fortune, you may not be able to drop $100 tips as often as I do, but you should tip fairly and generously when you get good service.

When my children were young, every year at Thanksgiving and Christmas I would get a few thousand dollars in twenty-dollar bills, and we would put the bills in envelopes. The kids and I would drive to an underprivileged section of town and just give the envelopes out to people at random. We didn't wait around to see what happened; we just handed out the money and left. We would go to shelters like the Salvation Army where they would be serving holiday meals and put envelopes containing money at each place on the tables. And again, we left quickly. For my kids, I wanted the focus to be on the act of giving, not on getting thanked.

I support and take pleasure in the concept of random acts of kindness. It's a wonderful way to make a positive difference in the world.

## More Than Money: Give Yourself

I know that the money I give away does a lot of good, but I can't put a price tag on the value of the time I spend with at-risk kids.

For example, I visit the Last Chance Ranch, a rural lockup in Glades County for some of Florida's most violent youthful offenders. I can talk to these boys from a place they understand, because I was a youthful offender. I tell them about my childhood, about my troubled teen years, and how I ended up in serious trouble and spent time in jail. And then I tell them how I turned my life around and how they can do it, too. I connect with them in a way that many people can't, because I've been where they are.

Because of what I have achieved in the business world, I feel I have a lot to offer organizations in the way of advice and guidance. That's why I serve on the board of directors of the Cape Coral Youth Center and other organizations. I am selective about volunteering my time in this way, because it is a serious commitment. When an organization gets me on its board, it gets more than just my name on the letterhead—it gets my energy and experience as well.

The millionaire mindset is one of personal and financial generosity, and of genuine caring. Good stewardship of your own gifts means giving a portion of them away—and doing that in a way that will make a positive difference.

# CHAPTER 21

# Your Personal
# Financial Strategy

I t's a lot easier to become a millionaire than it is to stay a millionaire. Making money is not as difficult as many people think it is, but once you have it, you need to manage it properly if you're going to keep it and make it grow. From the very beginning of your wealth-building journey, you need sound personal economic strategies to secure your financial future independent of any of your business activities.

By the way, the term "millionaire" is becoming passé. Bankers have created a new language called "wealth-speak." Individuals with more than $1 million in financial assets are no longer called millionaires (even though that's what they are), they're called HNWIs, or "high net worth individuals." Those with assets ranging from $500,000 to $1 million are the "mass affluent." Of course, it really doesn't matter if you're called a millionaire or an HNWI—what matters is that you achieve your financial goals.

Just a generation or so ago, the typical American family lived on one income, or perhaps one and a half, with one spouse working full-time and the other part-time. Today, most two-parent families are dual-income families, and even with two working adults, they're struggling to get by. This may describe you, or you may be in either better or worse shape than the "typical" family—it's not important where you are today, it's important that you believe you can develop the millionaire mindset and build and secure a fortune bigger than you ever dreamed.

## Protect Your Credit

Your personal credit rating is one of the most important financial assets you have—it's your financial reputation. While it's true that many a millionaire and even some billionaires have filed for bankruptcy protection and some have even gone bankrupt, lost everything, and rebuilt, it's always easier to build wealth if your credit is A+.

If you have limited or poor credit, take steps immediately to correct it. I explain in great detail how to do this in my book, *Credit: How to Obtain, Increase, and Preserve Credit.* If you have good credit, continue to build it and protect it by paying your bills on time and by checking your credit report at least once a year to be sure everything in it is accurate. Remember, credit reporting agencies make mistakes, and identity theft is a real and serious crime that causes major problems for victims. You could be doing everything right and still be denied credit because of something that wasn't your fault.

## What to Buy When You Get Some Cash

It's understandable that once you start to accumulate some cash you'll want to spend it on some luxuries. Resist that urge until you have built up some serious wealth, or at least until you have acquired some appreciating assets like real estate that are throwing off positive cash flow. Most things we consider luxuries are consumer purchases such as cars, entertainment, electronic gadgets, furniture, clothes, and jewelry—all depreciating assets that lose a substantial portion of their value the day you bring them home. When you have appreciating assets that are generating positive cash flow, you can use that money to buy the depreciating assets.

When you have the millionaire mindset, you'll spend your money on appreciating assets—things that will increase in value—especially in your early wealth-building days.

*During your early wealth-building days, spend your money on things that will increase in value.*

When I netted $11,000 cash on my first real estate investment, as I discussed earlier, I wasn't tempted to spend part of that $11,000 on clothes or a fancy night out on the town to celebrate. Why? Even though I didn't completely realize it at the time, I had the millionaire mindset. I knew that if I was going to achieve my financial goals, I had to take every penny from that first deal and reinvest it in more real estate.

It was years before I was comfortable spending money on nonessential consumer goods. In fact, I didn't even buy my first new car until years after I had reached a net worth of $1 million.

I did, however, buy a new small truck within the first couple of years of investing in real estate. It was necessary to effectively maintain and manage my rental units. While it was new, it wasn't anything that could be even remotely considered a luxury vehicle. I used a line of credit to make the purchase and let the cash flow from my properties make the payments.

When I finally decided to indulge in a new car, I was twenty-nine, and the car was a Porsche 944. It was beautiful—white with a custom red leather interior and loaded with extras. And just as an aside: I got taken to the cleaners on the deal. I leased it, and the salesman totally sucked me in. At the end of the lease, I was completely upside down (meaning that the car was worth much less than what I owed on it). But I loved the car, and I was making enough money that it wasn't a problem. And that's my point: I may have spent far more on that car than it was worth, but I was spending cash I had already earned, not racking up debt on a depreciating asset.

*People with the millionaire mindset consistently live below their means.*

My strategy—and self-discipline—paid off. Today, my wife and I enjoy a luxurious lifestyle that we can easily afford because we didn't waste our money on depreciating assets in our early years of wealth-building.

## Live Below Your Means

A mortgage company commercial features a guy on his riding lawn mower listing all the things he has: big house, new cars, country club membership, and more. As the commercial ends, he says, "How do I do it? I'm in debt up to my eyeballs. Somebody please help me."

It's sad but true that this fictitious character is typical of so many people who are living far beyond their means because they couldn't wait until they actually were wealthy before they started living that way.

People with the millionaire mindset consistently live *below* their means. It's not that they don't live comfortably, but they consistently spend less than they can afford.

My wife and I now live in a 16,000-square-foot mansion, our dream home. We spent years planning it. But we didn't break ground on it until several years after we could have, because we refuse to live at or beyond our means.

## Manage Your Assets

Asset management is knowing what you have and keeping it working for you. As you begin to build your portfolio and increase your assets, you would be wise to seek professional advice in this area. I stay actively involved in the management of my personal portfolio, but I still have a financial advisor who does research and makes recommendations on how I should allocate my resources.

A good financial advisor will not suggest any investment until he has evaluated your goals and your risk tolerance. Risk tolerance is a measure of your personal comfort with risk, and it is closely tied to your objectives and timeline. Typically, the younger you are, the more risk you're willing to take, because you have time to recover if something doesn't perform as expected. But you also have to keep your own personality in mind. Some people take a very conservative, safe approach to investing, regardless of their age. And some people take financial risks well into their sixties and seventies and beyond. Your financial advisor should take the time to understand how you operate and what you want to accomplish before making any recommendations.

*Calculate your net worth at least once a year.*

Real estate is, in my opinion, the fastest and easiest way to build wealth. But it's not the only asset class, and the millionaire mindset understands the value of diversification when it comes to investments. Get a good financial advisor to help you consider a range of portfolio mixes. Many investments are cyclical, and various asset classes perform better under certain conditions. Your financial advisor should understand this and be able to explain it to you.

Your financial advisor also needs to look at your entire net worth. He needs to know about and monitor all of your assets, even those he is not managing. Without that knowledge, he can't give you the best advice. And if all he wants to know about are the assets he's getting paid to manage, find another advisor.

To find a good financial advisor, start by talking to people you know and are comfortable with who are successful, and find out whom they use. Asking successful people for a referral just makes sense—you don't need investment advice from a failure. Asking people you are comfortable with also makes sense—these are the people who are likely to have similar goals and degrees of risk tolerance, which means they are likely to have a financial advisor you can relate to. When you ask for the referral, be sure to find out what they like and don't like about the advisor they use.

Call the advisor and schedule an initial interview. This should be a long-term relationship, so take the time up front to get to know and be sure you feel comfortable with this person. The advisor also needs to be able to relate to you and understand what you're doing. And if you don't have a lot of cash to invest right now, he needs to be excited about being part of your team as you grow your wealth. Keep in mind that some advisors will work only with clients who are investing large sums of money; it's as important that you meet your advisor's criteria as it is for him to meet yours.

Find out how the advisor generates his income. Is he commission-based or fee-based? One is not necessarily better or worse than the other, but you need to know—and you need to be sure your advisor is sitting on the same side of the table that you are.

There are financial advisors out there who charge just a planning fee to evaluate your situation and tell you what to do on a one-time basis. They tout their objectivity as an advantage—after all, they make the same amount of money regardless of what you end up doing. I recommend avoiding these planners. You want an advisor who is in the business of implementing and managing portfolios, one who is going to stick around and help you build your wealth for years to come.

One of my financial advisors says he looks at his clients as the CEOs and himself as their CFO. He does the research, keeps track of things, makes suggestions—but the final decision belongs to the client. He also says that a good investment advisor sits in the background but is nobody's yes-person. He tells me when he thinks I'm making a mistake, and I appreciate his honesty and forthrightness. But as he says, the final decision is mine.

Your financial advisor should be evaluating your entire portfolio on at least a quarterly basis and making asset-reallocation recommendations as appropriate and necessary. You should review it once a year to make sure you're on track with your game plan.

## What Are You Worth?

Calculate your net worth—basically, your assets minus your liabilities—at least once a year. The exercise will tell you where you are in relation to your goals, and also force you to look at your assets and determine if they are working as hard as they can for you. If you are managing your finances and investing wisely, it's entirely possible for you to have a higher net worth than someone living a far more luxurious lifestyle.

You need to keep a certain amount of cash in a savings account (or money market or other short-term, immediate-access account) so you have quick access to funds in an emergency. How much depends on your particular situation. Traditional financial wisdom says to have enough cash to cover three months of personal expenses. You should also have enough cash to cover six to twelve months of business expenses if something should happen and for some reason you have no revenue. But when you have more cash than whatever that designated emergency amount is, you need to invest it in a higher-yielding vehicle, even if it is not as liquid as a traditional savings account.

For purposes of net worth calculation, you don't need to distinguish between types of assets and liabilities. However, for your own financial management and planning, you need to be aware of the difference between liquid and nonliquid assets, as well as immediate liabilities and long-term debt. Liquid assets are cash or something of significant value that can be sold or otherwise turned into cash quickly. Nonliquid assets are accounts or other items of significant value that cannot be sold quickly, or if they are, would be subject to penalty. Immediate liabilities are debts you must repay within two years, such as automobile loans and credit cards. Long-term debt is payable over a longer period and typically includes real estate and business loans.

## A Special Piece of Property

I've already told you to never get emotionally involved with your real estate investments, but that's advice worth repeating. When you get emotional, you are more likely to make mistakes and do things that will cost you unnecessarily.

There is one piece of property that you probably won't be able to help getting emotional about, and that's your home. Our homes say a lot about who we are, and it's understandable if you don't look at

## Net Worth Calculation Worksheet

Date _____

**Assets**

Cash in personal bank accounts (checking, savings, money market) _____

Certificates of deposit, bonds, money market mutual funds, etc. _____

Stocks and stock market mutual funds _____

**Liquid Assets** _____

Personal real estate (home, vacation home) _____

Real estate investments _____

Business interests (company ownership or partial ownership) _____

Retirement-plan investments _____

Cash value of life insurance _____

Personal property (resale value) _____

Other assets _____

**Nonliquid Assets** _____

**Total Assets** _____

**Liabilities**

Automobile loans _____

Student loans _____

Credit card balances _____

Other short-term loans _____

Current bills and obligations _____

**Immediate Liabilities** _____

Mortgages _____

Other long-term debt _____

**Long-term Liabilities** _____

**Total Liabilities** _____

**Net Worth (total assets minus total liabilities)** _____

your own house through investor eyes. At the same time, you should always know the value of your own home—even though you may have no intention of selling it for years. Also, as you start to make money, be careful not to over-improve your home.

It may be tempting to over-improve and create the nicest house in the neighborhood. But if you do that, you may find the property hard to sell, because nobody wants to buy the most expensive house on the block. Generally, people want to buy on the low end and force the value up by making their own improvements. Certainly, make your house what you want and create a place where you'll enjoy living, but always keep resale in mind.

When I built my dream home, I wanted a spacious room for my home office with lots of built-in bookshelves and a fireplace. I know that I'm not going to live in that house forever, and at some point, a future owner may want to use that room for something other than an office—maybe a bedroom or a nursery. So even though I personally didn't need a full bath in my home office, I had one put in anyway. That's the way you should think as you're improving your home; do what you want and can afford, but also think about what a future owner might want.

## Estate Planning

There's an old line that everybody wants to go to heaven, but nobody wants to have to die to get there. Certainly, no one likes to think about dying, but the fact is that it happens to everybody. If you have worked hard and built your own personal fortune, take steps now to make sure that it's protected after you die. And if you're just getting started on your financial goals, make estate planning part of the process.

An estate is the total property, including all assets and liabilities, that an individual owned prior to the distribution of that property under the terms of a will, trust, or inheritance laws. Property is either real or personal. Real property is real estate; personal property is everything else, including physical assets and financial property such as cash, bank accounts, securities, receivables, and insurance policies.

Everyone does estate planning, either on purpose or by default. If you create a will and set up trusts that provide instructions for the distribution of your estate to your heirs, you've done active, purposeful estate planning. If you don't have a will and don't bother setting up trusts, that's estate planning by default, because the inheritance laws of your state will control the distribution of your estate. Each state has formulas and rules for moving assets to heirs, and these may not be what you would have done. And if you have no heirs who fit the state's definition, your assets will be taken by the state.

*Control the assets left after you die with careful estate planning.*

The state's legal procedure for identifying your rightful heirs and getting the legal title of the property out of your name and into their name(s) is called probate. An estate must be above a certain size specified by the state before it is required to go through the probate process. Probate can be time-consuming and expensive, often costing anywhere from 6 to 10 percent of the value of the estate. That means even a modest estate of $250,000 could run as much as $15,000 to $25,000 to probate—and in my opinion, that's a shameful waste of money. Also, it's not uncommon for probate to lead to family battles and lengthy litigation—and all probate procedures are public, which means family privacy is lost. Clearly, avoiding probate is the best strategy.

You can avoid probate by placing your assets in a trust before your death. Depending on your particular assets, you may want to create more than one trust for different assets—especially if you have assets such as real estate in multiple states, where the laws governing trusts may be different.

A trust is a legal entity created by a contract between two parties for the benefit of a third party. The first party is the grantor, which is the individual(s) who owns the property being transferred into the trust. The second is the trustee, which is the legal administrator of the trust. The third party is the beneficiary, which is the individual(s) or organization(s) that receives benefits or income from the trust property.

Though the trust is the legal owner of the property for title-transfer purposes, as the grantor, you can retain complete control of and benefits from the property during your life, and the beneficiaries will receive their benefits after your death.

I'm going to assume that you're reading this book because you want to become wealthy (or wealthier). In that case, chances are excellent that you will die with an estate large enough to qualify for probate—unless you put the majority of your assets into trusts.

Even if most of your assets are in trusts, you probably need a will. If you have minor children, you definitely need a will. In addition to directing the disposition of your property, your will should name guardians for your children and their property.

When creating your will and setting up trusts, consult with a qualified attorney who specializes in estate planning. And always read your will and any trust documents before signing them. All law offices use templates when creating these routine documents. There's nothing wrong with that, but editing mistakes can occur, and you don't want to run into a problem later because you missed an error when you signed the document.

It's important to understand that there is a big difference between avoiding probate costs (important) and reducing taxes (perhaps even more important). Trusts are a great way to do both, but they must be set up properly in accordance with all applicable state laws and federal regulations.

Estate planning is not something you can just do once and forget about. As your assets grow and as your family situation changes (marriages, divorces, births, deaths, moving to a different state or country), you'll need to review your estate plan and make any appropriate changes.

## Write an Ethical Will

An ethical will isn't a legal document, nor does it have anything to do with estate planning, but the process of organizing your assets and articulating your wishes for what's to happen to them when you die may prompt you to write an ethical will. Ethical wills are more of a spiritual legacy than a material one. They're a way for you to express your love and affection, to share your values and beliefs, to pass on the life lessons you have learned as well as your hopes and dreams for the future.

Ethical wills have been around since ancient times. In Genesis 49, Jacob speaks an ethical will for his sons on his deathbed. Chapters 15–18 of the Gospel of John include an oral ethical will from Jesus to the disciples as the time of His crucifixion draws near. Ethical wills have evolved from statements made at the end of one's life to written documents created by individuals at turning points in their lives and shared with family and friends prior to the writer's death.

A great Web site devoted to ethical wills (www.ethicalwill.com) was created by Barry K. Baines, M.D. There, Baines says that ethical wills may be one of the most cherished and meaningful gifts you can leave to your family and community. The occasions when you might consider writing an ethical will include when a couple becomes engaged; when you are expecting a baby; when a couple divorces; and other significant life milestones. Many people use ethical wills to articulate the reasons behind estate-planning decisions, such as why a particular family member's inheritance was handled in a specific way. Formal estate-planning instruments rarely include much in the way of explanations, and this is your chance to let your heirs know why you did things as you did.

## Asset Protection

As important as planning for the disposition and disbursement of your assets on your death is making sure those assets are protected while you are alive. The wealthy have practiced asset protection for decades; the process includes totally legal and ethical strategies to protect the assets you work so hard to accumulate.

Why do you need asset protection? For starters, nine out of every ten lawsuits in the world are filed in the United States, and every year, one out of ten Americans is sued. The more money you have, and the more complex your business is, the more likely you are to be sued. And simply forming a corporation—although that is a key component of a sound asset-protection strategy—is not enough.

Let me stress that I believe you should always pay your just debts. Do not use asset protection to avoid legitimate obligations. While that's certainly possible and may even be legal, it's morally wrong—and it will catch up with you.

Asset protection should be an integrated part of your overall personal and business financial strategy, as well as your estate plan.

The key to effective asset protection is to implement your plan *before* you need it. Once you have been served with a lawsuit or otherwise become aware that you are a target of a claim, any effort to shield your assets may be viewed as fraudulent conveyance and could be subject to civil and criminal penalties.

When someone wins a lawsuit and obtains a judgment against you, he becomes what is called a judgment creditor. If you don't pay him, he can go after your assets. But he can't take what you don't own, and he won't try to get what he doesn't know about.

The primary goals of a sound asset-protection strategy are: privacy, so that the details of the ownership of your assets are not available through public records; control, so you can maintain control of your assets even if you have been sued or a judgment has been entered against you, your company, or any property you own; and liability protection.

## The Best Way to Own Real Estate

Never own real estate in your own name. If you do, that information will show up in public records for anyone to see. More important, any judgment against you can turn into a lien against *all* your property. If the judgment is valid, you should pay it. But if you disagree with it and appeal it, you will still have a lien on your property while the appeal is pending, and that means you do not have control over your own assets.

It's a good general rule to own each of your real estate and other investments in a separate trust. For example, it would be foolish of me to have my construction company and my land development company owned by the same entity. They are completely and totally separate. Each of my real estate investments is in a separate land trust, and I recommend you use this same strategy.

Setting up a land trust is not complicated. You need to designate a trustee, which is the person whose name is in the public records. Your land trust agreement will also name a beneficiary—that's you or your company. The beneficiary directs the trustee (although in most cases you won't tell the trustee to do anything at all), manages and controls the property, and gets the money. This is all done through a private contract that does not need to be recorded in the public records. All you need to do is change the title of the property from the previous owner to the trustee as the agent of the trust.

*Never own real estate in your own name; use land trusts.*

Here's how it works: You decide to buy a ten-acre tract of land that you intend to develop into a small commercial center. You establish a revocable land trust by creating a land trust agreement and name your married sister (who does not have the same last name that you do) as trustee and you as beneficiary. Because the trust is revocable, you can amend or terminate it at any point. When you close on the sale and transfer ownership from the seller, the title lists the new owners as the trust, and your sister will sign the closing documents as the trustee. Only you and the trustee know who the real owner is, and you should include a provision in the trust agreement that explicitly prevents the trustee from disclosing your interest in the property.

I recommend naming the trusts with the address of the property or some other similar common identifier. A house at 456 Main St. would be placed in the 456 Main St. Land Trust; an apartment complex named Shady Oaks would be placed in the Shady Oaks Apartments Land Trust; a vacant lot at the intersection of Broadway and First Street would be placed in the Broadway-First Land Trust. Keep it simple.

Land trusts are legal in all fifty states and Canada, but not all lawyers are familiar with them. Also, there are some particular issues in Pennsylvania which makes owning property in land trusts not the best strategy in that state. Wherever you live, seek out a lawyer who understands land trusts so that you are sure you are making the best decision based on your circumstances and the laws of your state. While you don't need an attorney to create a land trust, it's a good idea to have your contracts reviewed by one before you sign them—and the attorney should understand what you're doing. You may have to shop around for a lawyer who is familiar with land trusts, but it's worth the time and effort.

Placing every investment into a separate land trust takes just a little bit of time and effort, and the benefits are worth it. Consider this scenario: You own all your property in your name, and your assets consist of four duplexes, a twenty-four-unit apartment building, and two small retail shopping centers. One of the tenants in the apartment building slips on a sidewalk, sues you, and wins a judgment against you. That judgment becomes a lien on *all* your properties, not just the one where the tenant was injured. And if you don't pay the judgment, the lienholder can force the sale of your properties until the judgment is satisfied. But if each of these properties is owned by a separate land trust, the tenant would have sued the owner of the apartment building, and the judgment would become a lien against that property alone. Your other properties are safe, and you are free to sell or mortgage them as you choose. Certainly, if the judgment is legal, and if you have exhausted all possible appeals, you need to pay it. But you want to make the payment on your terms, not on the terms of the lienholder. You don't want to be forced to sell your assets when it would be better to get the cash another way.

## Avoiding the Sharks

Lawyers like to go after "deep pockets"—if they think you have money, you're more likely to be sued. One way to avoid that would be to live very modestly. While I recommend that in your early stages of wealth-building—not for asset protection but to accumulate wealth as quickly as possible—it's understandable that you'll want to live a comfortable and even luxurious lifestyle when you can afford it. Just keep as low a profile as possible and don't title your assets in your own name.

Another important element of asset protection is insurance— not only to pay any potential judgments, but also because most insurance policies require the insurer to provide a defense if you are sued, whether or not the suit has merit. So let the insurance company pay your legal expenses and handle any liability lawsuits.

In addition to the risks created by litigation, use asset-protection strategies to reduce your tax liability. Understand that there is a big difference between legitimate tax reduction (which is legal) and tax avoidance or nonpayment (which is not). If you are making money, you cannot avoid income taxes—but you can structure your businesses and investments to reduce the amount of tax you have to pay.

Asset protection is not a do-it-yourself project. It's a good idea to consult with an expert, who should have extensive tax and international law training. Always check references and make sure you completely understand the recommended strategies.

John D. Rockefeller once said, "Own nothing and control everything." That is the essence of asset protection.

▼

# CHAPTER 22

# The Final Chapter:
# Your Beginning

T hat you've made it to this chapter tells me that you either have the millionaire mindset, or you're well on your way to acquiring it. Congratulations!

Of course, the real work begins when you put this book down and start applying what you've learned. Developing the millionaire mindset is simple, but it's not as easy as taking a magic pill.

By simple, I mean that if you understand the principles, you can put together a plan that will take you to your goals. But it's not easy, and it's not magic—it's work and discipline.

It means you have to overcome your own fear of failure—and your own fear of success. You need to get around the roadblocks thrown up by the people who tell you that your plans won't work. And you need to keep going even after you've heard the word "no" so many times that you've lost count. Australian businessman Barry Bull once said, "Never give up. Realize that when you face problems, you are almost there. 'No' is negotiable. Ninety percent of people give up when they are 10 percent from achieving their goals. The word that stops them is 'no.'"

Problems can't stop you from turning your dreams into reality. Roadblocks can't stop you. Your friends, relatives, and acquaintances can't stop you. You are the only person who can stop you from succeeding. And you—with the millionaire mindset—are the only person who can make you succeed.

## Move Quickly

The advice to start small and grow is generally good advice. But the key word there is *grow*. It's too easy to get to a level that's comfortable and get stuck. Once you've got some success under your belt, continue to push yourself on to bigger and better things.

*You are the only person who can stop you from succeeding.*

I've probably made more money in the last three years than I did in my first ten or fifteen years combined, and I did it because I was willing to go for the big money—and so should you. I always keep an open mind, I'm receptive to new ideas, new strategies, and I am willing to take smart, calculated risks.

Develop a strategic plan that will get you where you want to be in the quickest amount of time—then enjoy the fruits of your labors.

As St. Francis of Assisi once said, "Start by doing what's necessary, then what's possible, and suddenly you are doing the impossible."

If you knew me thirty years ago—a troubled high school dropout with a bad attitude—and someone suggested that one day I would be a multimillionaire heading up dozens of companies, including an international training and education company teaching others how to become wealthy, you probably would have said, "Impossible." But I did what was necessary, and it became possible.

## Maximize Your Time

There are twenty-four hours in every day. Period. That's it. That's all you get, that's all I get. And no matter how wealthy you become, you can't change that.

Time is the most precious commodity you have—treat it like that, and don't squander it. One of the nice things about money is that you can always make more of it, but that's not so with time. If

*Time is the most precious commodity you have—don't squander it.*

I make an investment that heads south and costs me money, it may bother me, but I don't dwell on it. I know I can find another investment that will make up what I lost and then some.

Let me offer you two pieces of advice on the bad deals you do and the ones you pass by. First, understand that some of your best deals will be the ones you don't do. It's better to not do a deal than to struggle through a deal with a lot of hassle that ends up costing you money. Second, recognize that you can't make a bad deal good by hanging on to it. If you've made a mistake, get out of the deal—at a loss if you have to—and move on.

Remember, once time has passed, it's gone. You can't get it back.

I've always thought the phrase "time management" was a misnomer. You can't manage time—but you can manage yourself in a way that maximizes your time.

## Invest in Yourself

You and what you know are the most valuable assets you have. Always be investing in yourself, and you'll always be increasing your value.

One of my students attended our basic three-day real estate

investment training and decided he didn't need any additional classes. He thought the training was too expensive and that he could be successful with the knowledge he had. He put together a plan and got out there and worked hard—and didn't manage to close a single deal. After a few months, he spoke with one of our counselors and decided to invest in some advanced training. Immediately after his first advanced training course, he closed on a deal that netted him more than $60,000 profit—and he did it without investing a dime of his own money.

With education, as with just about everything in life, you get what you pay for. You must be willing to invest in your education so you can learn what you need to reach your goals.

Do you know what they call a doctor who graduated from Harvard Medical School with an A average?

Doctor.

Do you know what they call a doctor who graduated from a medical school in Grenada with a C average?

Doctor.

The question is, which would you rather go to when you're sick?

If you're going to be an investor, whether it's real estate, stock trading, or something else, you need the best education possible. And if you're not willing to get it, get a job as a laborer where you don't need an education.

When you educate yourself and do the business correctly, the money follows.

## Do the Work

You can't buy a book or a course on real estate, put it under your pillow and sleep on it, and wake up to find a duplex in the driveway. It's just not going to happen.

Remember, the only place where success comes before work is in the dictionary.

## Study Other Millionaires

Are the rich different, as F. Scott Fitzgerald wrote? Indeed they are. And it's not just because, as Ernest Hemingway said, "Yes, they have more money." It's *why* and *how* they have more money. And it's because they have the millionaire mindset.

*Keep your eye on where you're going, not where you've been.*

Starting today and for the rest of your life, study successful people. Read the biographies and autobiographies of millionaires, multimillionaires, and billionaires in every industry.

Can you learn something from Donald Trump, who was the son of a wealthy man, even though you're starting with nothing? Sure. Can you learn something from Bill Gates, even though the only thing you know about computers is how to send e-mail? Of course. Can you learn something from Bill Marriott, even though you have absolutely no interest in the hospitality industry? Definitely.

My personal library includes books either by or about hundreds of entrepreneurs, successful businesspeople, leaders of corporate America, great religious leaders, and savvy politicians. I also have hundreds of books on marketing, business, speaking, and writing. And I have learned something worthwhile from every book I've read.

## ID Check

Start thinking in terms of what and where you want to be, not what and where you are now. When someone asks you what you do, what do you say? That you work for the phone company or the post office or whatever? Or that you're *trying* to be an investor? When you have the millionaire mindset, you will confidently say that you are an investor—whether or not you've actually closed on a transaction. That confidence will help you move toward your goals.

Remember, success breeds success. The more successful you are, the more successful you will become, the easier the deals will be, and the more choices you will have. Keep your eye on where you're going, not where you've been.

## The Final Question

I began this book with the question: Why isn't everyone rich? Then I took it down to a more personal level: If you are not as wealthy as you'd like to be, why not?

By now you know the answer. You understand the millionaire mindset and you know how to develop it for yourself.

I'm going to close this book with a few more questions: Are you a winner? Do you want to live a life of adventure, achievement, and excitement? If so, when will you start? Now? And if not now, when?

I've shown you how to become a winner and accomplish all of your goals. Your future is now up to you. Just do it.

# Appendix A

## Resources

*Investment training resources available through:*

Wealth Intelligence Academy™
1612 East Cape Coral Parkway
Cape Coral, FL 33904
1-800-737-9533
www.wiacademy.com

## Real Estate Investing

*Intensified Real Estate Training:* A three-day, hands-on program that teaches how to find investment properties, how to talk to sellers, how to finance purchases, how to build a professional support team (a Power Team), and includes a field trip where students often make offers on properties.

*Wholesale Buying:* Students learn to locate, evaluate, and negotiate for wholesale properties; how to find owners of vacant properties; how to assign contracts and set up double closings; and how to develop profitable exit strategies.

*Foreclosure Training:* During this intense three-day program, students learn foreclosure basics and strategies, how to find foreclosures and make contact with owners, how to determine values and create a profitable deal, how to buy at auction, and more.

*Purchase Option:* These solid, proven strategies show students how to control property without buying it, how to buy with little or no money down, and how to maximize your cash flow with a variety of creative techniques.

*Property Management and Cash Flow:* A three-day comprehensive course in property management that includes how to acquire property, legal issues, evictions, risk management, tenant and landlord rights and responsibilities, taxes, rental subsidies, and more.

*Commercial Real Estate Investing:* Students learn how to locate and determine value of commercial properties, the ins and outs of commercial leases, and how to profitably manage commercial real estate.

*Keys to Creative Real Estate Financing:* This three-day training program shows students how to structure financing with bad credit or no credit, prepare and present a powerful financial statement, work with a mortgage broker, work with bank lenders, work with hard money lenders, create a mortgage, and more.

*Manufactured/Mobile Homes & RV Parks:* Students learn how to develop and operate a manufactured/mobile home or RV park; how to buy, sell, and rent existing manufactured/mobile homes; how to get bargains through foreclosures and repossessions; how to line up regular and unconventional financing; and more.

*Rehabbing for Profit:* A real-life, "get your hands dirty" training program that teaches students how to plan the job; create a cost estimate and timeline; streamline the permitting process; understand codes, zoning, insurance, and risk; when to do it yourself and when to hire someone; and more.

*Asset Protection and Tax Relief:* Students learn to develop a personal, step-by-step plan to protect both business and personal assets, reduce income taxes, and eliminate estate taxes.

*Discount Notes & Mortgages:* Students learn how the cash flow industry in general and the discount notes and mortgages business in particular can help build wealth and enhance real estate investing.

*International Finance and Investment:* In a luxurious week in Costa Rica, students learn how to invest in foreign real estate; how to take advantage of regulatory arbitrage; how to invest in international mutual funds; how to build an offshore Power Team; how to develop and implement multijurisdictional strategies for true asset protections; and they have the opportunity to network with some of the world's best international finance and investment planners and practitioners.

*Land Investing and Development:* Students learn how to invest in vacant land, create value, make a market, control value, and create pricing.

## Stock Market Investing

*Master Trader:* Students receive a complete foundation of practical advanced technical analysis. They learn ideal trends and topping/bottoming characteristics; swing and position trading; exiting guidelines and a refined stop-adjustment strategy; and more.

*Trading P.I.T.:* This three-day program shows students how to master bidirectional trading and profit whether the stock goes up or down; how to successfully hedge trades; how to increase profit potential through the power of online resources; how to enter and exit a trade with strategies used by professionals; and more.

*Advanced P.I.T.:* Building on the Trading P.I.T. course, this program teaches students nine advanced spread strategies; how to lock in on winning trades and adjust underperforming ones; how to flip from bullish to bearish and vice versa on open positions; and more.

*H.I.T.S. (Hedging and Institutional Tactics and Strategies):* This program covers revolutionary new tools, including single stock futures, indices, and ETFs, and keeps students "in the know" with the latest trading developments.

*The Trading Room:* In this unique program, trading principles are taught and applied to live market scenarios as a group or individually, depending on the student's risk parameters.

*Advanced Covered Calls:* Students learn to generate reliable, predictable, consistent monthly cash flow by writing calls and puts while building a highly profitable stock portfolio.

*Home-study programs available through:* www.russwhitney.com.

*Building Wealth™ Home Study Course:* The home-study version of Russ Whitney's Millionaire U Advanced Training. Package includes manuals, software, videotapes, and CDs taken from the heart of Russ's live training.

*One-in-a-Million 90-Day Challenge:* The plan and tools necessary to break the chains that have held you back so that you can achieve your goals, win at the game of life, and build your own personal fortune.

*Overcoming the Hurdles & Pitfalls of Real Estate Investing:* Russ Whitney's first book, outlining his early days as a real estate investor and how he went from being a laborer to one of America's youngest self-made millionaires.

# Appendix B

## Sample Rental Application

Please complete the entire application and submit with a copy of your driver's license or identification card, a copy of your Social Security card, and a copy of a payroll check stub.

Name _____

Current address _____

City _____ State _____ Zip _____

Telephone (Home) _____ (Work) _____

Fax _____ Cell phone _____

Pager _____ E-mail _____

Social Security Number _____

Driver's License Number _____ State _____

Occupants (list each occupant, including children)

Name _____ Relationship _____ Age _____

Name _____ Relationship _____ Age _____

Name _____ Relationship _____ Age _____

Name _____ Relationship _____ Age _____

Name _____ Relationship _____ Age _____

Current landlord _____ Telephone _____

How long? _____ Monthly rent _____

Reason for leaving _____

Previous landlord (if less than 3 years) _____ Telephone _____

Previous address _____

City _____ State _____ Zip _____

How long? _____ Monthly rent _____

Reason for leaving _____

Employer _____

Address _____

City_____ State _____ Zip _____

Telephone _____

Your position _____ How long _____

Supervisor _____ Title _____

Gross salary/income _____ per week   two weeks   month (circle one)

Take home _____ per week   two weeks   month (circle one)


Previous employer (if less than 3 years) _____

Address _____

City_____ State _____ Zip _____

Telephone _____

Your position _____ How long _____

Supervisor _____ Title _____

Gross salary/income _____ per week   two weeks   month (circle one)

Take home _____ per week   two weeks   month (circle one)


Additional employment information

Employer _____

Address _____

City_____ State _____ Zip _____

Telephone _____

Your position _____ How long _____

Supervisor _____ Title _____

Gross salary/income _____ per week   two weeks   month (circle one)

Take home _____ per week   two weeks   month (circle one)

Emergency contact information (please provide two emergency contacts, including nearest living relative)

Name _____ Relationship _____

Address _____

City _____ State _____ Zip _____

Telephone _____


Name _____ Relationship _____

Address _____

City _____ State _____ Zip _____

Telephone _____


Bank Name _____

Checking Account Number _____ Savings Account Number _____

Other income not listed _____ Source _____


Vehicles to be parked on property

Make _____ Model _____ Color _____ Year _____ License _____

Make _____ Model _____ Color _____ Year _____ License _____


Have you ever been evicted? _____ (if yes, please explain) _____

Have you ever broken a lease? _____ (if yes, please explain) _____


Applicant represents that the above information is true and complete, and authorizes verification.


_____          _____

Signature                                          Date

# Appendix C

## Sample Offer to Purchase Real Estate

Be it known that the undersigned, _____ (Buyer), offers to purchase from
your name followed by "and/or assigns"

_____ (Owner), real estate known as _____
name of seller/owner                                                    street address

in the City/Town of _____, County of _____, State of

_____, said property more particularly described as:

Legal description to be provided by closing agent.

The purchase price offered is:           $_____

Deposit herewith paid:                $_____

Balance due at closing:              $_____

Total purchase price:                $_____

This offer is conditional upon the following terms:

1. Said property is to be sold free and clear of all encumbrances, by good and marketable title, with full possession to said property available to Buyer at date of closing.

2. The closing shall occur on or about _____ at the closing agent office of
                                                       30 days of acceptance

_____ .
name and address of your closing agent

3. Subject to inspection and approval of bids by Buyer to be completed in writing with 14 business days; or, if the property is not vacant, within 14 business days after the property is vacated.

4. Buyer and Seller to pay normal closing costs; specific closing costs to be detailed on sales contract.

5. Seller to provide Buyer with access to property upon acceptance.

6. Other terms: _____

This offer shall remain open until _____ o'clock on _____ and if not accepted by said time, this offer shall be deemed rescinded and all deposits shall be refunded.

Seller's acknowledgement: _____ Date: _____

_____       _____
Buyer                                                    Date

_____       _____
Buyer                                                    Date

_____       _____
Owner                                                    Date

_____       _____
Owner                                                    Date

# Index

# Free
# Real Estate Workshop
# Certificate

As a thank you for purchasing *The Millionaire Real Estate Mindset*, Russ Whitney cordially invites **you and a guest** to attend a local **FREE Real Estate Workshop.**

Designed to keep you on track, moving towards your next important step - this motivational event will help you focus on your success goals.

At this workshop, a member of Russ' own Wealth Team will expand on the valuable insights provided in this book by discussing:

- What is missing in *your* real estate strategy
- How to break free of the fears that hold *you* back
- Investing strategies that work in *your* market
- Preparing yourself for the really BIG deals
- How *you* can invest in and develop raw land
- New international real estate investing options
- Building Wealth by changing *your* mindset

*"Keep your eye on where you are going, not where you have been."*
– Russ Whitney

To register for a FREE workshop in your area go to
**www.russwhitney.com/mindset/workshop**
Or call **1-877-296-4700**